D0146194

BESIEGED
BEDFELLOWS

Recent Titles in
Contributions in Political Science
Series Editor: Bernard K. Johnpoll

Ethnic Groups and U.S. Foreign Policy
Mohammed E. Ahrari, editor

Referendum Voting: Social Status and Policy Preferences
Harlan Hahn and Sheldon Kamieniecki

Ordered Liberty and the Constitutional Framework: The Political Thought of
Friedrech A. Hayek
Barbara M. Rowland

Policy Evaluation for Local Government
Terry Busson and Philip Coulter, editors

New Tides in the Pacific: Pacific Basin Cooperation and the Big Four
(Japan, PRC, USA, USSR)
Roy Kim and Hilary Conroy, editors

Campaigns in the News: Mass Media and Congressional Elections
Jan Pons Vermeer, editor

Cultural Policy and Socialist France
David Wachtel

Liberalization and Redemocratization in Latin America
George A. Lopez and Michael Stohl, editors

Terrible Beyond Endurance? The Foreign Policy of State Terrorism
Michael Stohl and George A. Lopez, editors

Adjusting the Balance: Federal Policy and Victim Services
Steven Rathgeb Smith and Susan Freinkel

U.S. Policy on Jerusalem
Yossi Feintuch

The Ethics of Public Service: Resolving Moral Dilemmas in Public
Organizations
Kathryn G. Denhardt

Politics Through a Looking-Glass: Understanding Political Cultures Through
a Structuralist Interpretation of Narratives
Eloise A. Buker

BESIEGED BEDFELLOWS

Israel and the Land of Apartheid

Benjamin M. Joseph

CONTRIBUTIONS IN POLITICAL SCIENCE,
NUMBER 199

GREENWOOD PRESS

New York · Westport, Connecticut · London

Library of Congress Cataloging-in-Publication Data

Joseph, Benjamin M. (Benjamin Manashe), 1954–
 Besieged bedfellows.

 (Contributions in political science, ISSN 0147-1066 ;
no. 199)
 Bibliography: p.
 Includes index.
 1. Israel—Relations—South Africa. 2. South
Africa—Relations—Israel. I. Title.
DS119.8.S6J67   1988   327.5694068   86-17733
ISBN 0-313-25461-3 (lib. bdg. : alk. paper)

British Library Cataloguing in Publication Data is available.

Library of Congress Catalog Card Number: 86-17733
ISBN: 0-313-25461-3
ISSN: 0147-1066

First published in 1988

Greenwood Press, Inc.
88 Post Road West, Westport, Connecticut 06881

Printed in the United States of America

∞

The paper used in this book complies with the
Permanent Paper Standard issued by the National
Information Standards Organization (Z39.48-1984).

10 9 8 7 6 5 4 3 2 1

Contents

Preface

This book deals with a manifold relationship, most aspects of which are classified or played down for reasons of state. No archival sources or other official materials are available, other than those distributed for public relations purposes. Thus it is not surprising to read a pledge by a former South African government official that "there is a lot about South Africa and Israel that I will never speak or write about"; the countries have a relationship that he describes as an "alliance." (Eschel Rhoodie, *The Real Information Scandal* [Pretoria: Orbis, 1983] p. 110). Or consider the carefully chosen words of Gad Yaakovi, presently Israeli Minister of Economics and Planning, who hailed his country's economic and "other" ties with South Africa in a television interview. (Yoav Karni, "Dr. Shekel and Mr. Apartheid," in *Yediot Aharonot*, March 13, 1983).

Most chapters in this book were completed before March 1987 when the Israeli government announced that it would not sign new military contracts with South Africa beyond those already in effect. The announcement was made days before the release of a U.S. State Department report mandated by Congress that named Israel as a major government-to-government arms partner of South Africa. By making the announcement, the Israeli government admitted what its spokesmen and supporters in the West had denied for nearly two decades. The carefully chosen language of the statement, its timing, and the record of the Israeli government suggested that the aim was first and foremost to impress U.S. Congressmen and Jewish leaders, while preserving the bulk of the existing relationship with South Africa. The background and significance of this announcement, as well as of the report to Congress, are discussed in greater detail in the epilogue.

Despite the secrecy and official evasions in the years in which this book was completed, every attempt was made to examine almost all publicly available materials in English, Hebrew, and translated Afrikaans. Few other writings on this subject have made extensive use of Israeli sources in Hebrew, which are least likely to be accused of reporting "PLO propaganda."

I was fortunate enough to write the book in New York City where I was able to take advantage of the data banks and combined research collections of the New York Public Library (including the Schomburg Center for Research in Black Culture), Columbia University and New York University. Other valuable materials were received, with the assistance of New York Public Library staff, from the Library of Congress, the Africana collection at Yale University, Northwestern University, and Cornell. The United Nations Centre Against Apartheid provided me with many reports on South African–Israeli relations, while the American Committee on Africa and the African-American Institute allowed me to use their files, which contain South African and African publications not available elsewhere in the area. Israeli materials were available at the Zionist Archives in New York City, the New York Public Library Jewish division and at the Jewish Theological Seminary.

The often-overlooked South African Jewish periodicals were among the most helpful sources of information. No other type of periodical reports more news about the progress of Israeli–South African relations. *Jewish Affairs*, published by the Board of Deputies, regularly reprints clippings on the subject from the South African press, including translations from Afrikaans.

A significant book, *The Unnatural Alliance*, was published in London in 1984. The author is James Adams, defense correspondent and senior executive with the *Sunday Times*. The information he gathered helped back up much of what had been previously reported about Israeli–South African military and nuclear ties. Other than South African and Israeli spokesmen, most reviewers accepted the findings of the book as generally reliable. A sample of the reviews can be found in the first footnote in the introductory chapter.

Dr. Benjamin Beit-Hallahmi of Haifa University, who has been closely following this relationship even longer than I have, made many helpful suggestions. The opportunity to compare notes with him has helped make this book better than it might otherwise be. In 1987 Dr. Beit-Hallahmi completed *The Israeli Connection: Who Israel Arms and Why* (New York: Pantheon). Though the author had no such goal in mind, the book comes close to being an encyclopaedia of Israeli business with and assistance to brutal regimes from Manila to Managua, and, not the least, South Africa.

And finally, a word about what can and cannot be expected from this work. Its purpose has been neither to catalogue every single detail, visit, or transaction in recent years, (in a few instances the reader who is interested in still more details on a given issue will be referred to other sources, such as *The Israeli Connection*), nor does this book attempt to compete with investigative journalism in uncovering "scoops" that are currently state secrets. One cannot emphasize enough that while the book attempts to bring together all that is currently known about Israeli–South African ties, the researcher is essentially limited to digging in the public record. On occasion, someone who has access to more restricted information may choose to confirm something already published or disclose something new, but this book, unlike *The Unnatural Alliance*, does not claim to rely on its own private sources.

It is also worth noting that since the topic here is South African–Israeli relations since the early 1970s, the reader should not expect a comprehensive history of Zionism, Israel, or South Africa, nor a full review of the issues, claims, and counterclaims in the Middle East conflict. Similarly, no justice can be done here to issues such as anti-Semitism, colonialism, racism, Israeli domestic politics, or ethnic divisions, to mention a few.

The discourse is, or at least was meant to be, matter-of-fact, without preaching or passing judgment on the wisdom and morality of the policies in question. It is left for the reader to judge, for instance, whether alternatives to close ties with South Africa may be available to Israeli leaders, and, if so, what those alternatives are.

BESIEGED
BEDFELLOWS

CHAPTER 1

Introduction

Soon after I began to research the topic of South African–Israeli relations, I became aware of an interesting pattern: When I would tell someone what I was writing about, the response would in many cases include an unsolicited defense or condemnation of the relationship. Of course, it's not a startling revelation that there is a wide range of emotions and convictions about Israel, South Africa, and the two together. This response does, however, serve as a reminder from the very start that no imaginable thesis is likely to satisfy all objections from all sides. By its nature, a project such as this runs more than a minor risk of being seen as "biased" or "polemical" by one side or the other.

For many in the West, the burgeoning links between Israel and South Africa have been highly "unnatural"; one of the more important books on the subject is the aforementioned *The Unnatural Alliance*.[1] There are not only the obvious disparities in economic power and size between two countries separated by the world's second largest continent. Perhaps more than anything else, those who are aware of and acknowledge the extent of the ties between these states are likely to point to the irony of the embrace between victims of racism on the one hand and a country with agencies for race classification on the other hand. The question goes like this: how can those who have experienced the most monstrous manifestation of racism in human history be the allies of a system with Nuremberg-style legislation and with leaders who distinguished themselves as Nazi sympathizers?

Few world issues come as close to an international consensus as rejection of apartheid. For the black majority, apartheid has meant race classification, forced resettlement in artificial "homelands," police shootings, pass laws (recently repealed), a lack of due process, and, in general, the status of aliens in their own land. Hence the daily demonstrations in front of South African embassies, sit-ins at universities, and persistent calls, some of which are beginning to bear fruit at this writing, for Western sanctions and divestment. For African states in particular, apartheid has been a fundamental concern since the beginning of independence and a reminder of how incomplete and fragile that independence is. The 1967 Kinshasa Resolution on Apartheid and Racial Discrimination adopted by the Assembly of Heads of State and Government, for instance, referred to the South African system as "an odious crime against humanity" and "a grave menace to peace and security."[2] Alliance or cooperation with apartheid does little to ease the concern and condemnation.

Israel's ties with South Africa have been repeatedly condemned by the General Assembly of the United Nations. The United Nations Centre Against Apartheid has regularly published detailed reports about the progress of the relationship, as it has done on occasion regarding the ties of other countries with South Africa. Archbishop Desmond Tutu is also on record with sharp criticism of Israel for this cooperation. In one instance he "chided the Israeli government for collaboration with South Africa, calling apartheid 'so reminiscent of Hitler's Aryan madness'." Tutu also deplored the treatment of Palestinians as something that in his view is "totally inconsistent with who she (Israel) is."[3] For many years the world-famous clergyman has declined invitations to visit Israel.

Israel's close ties with South Africa have been an embarrassment to many Jews in the United States as well, especially those who favor Western divestment. Firm supporters of Israel who abhor South African apartheid are likely to insist that the relationship has been greatly exaggerated. Along with Israeli spokesmen, they point to declared statistics on trade and charge that a double standard is being applied: by comparison with other Western countries or black Africa, it is argued, Israel's dealings with South Africa are miniscule and certainly do not imply approval of that country's domestic policies. It is similarly pointed out that most of South Africa's oil is supplied by "the Arabs," a reference to oil of Middle Eastern origin that reaches South Africa, usually through Western shippers and traders. In short, much of the discussion of South African–Israeli ties continues to revolve around defense and condemnation. We'll return to this question in a later chapter.

An *alliance*? In a 1984 review article, the editors of the *Sunday Times* of London described the Israeli–South African connection as a "major new force on the world scene."[4] In many of the writings on the subject, the relationship is described as an "alliance," as a quick look at the bibliography can reveal. At least one former high official, South African Secretary for Information Eschel Rhoodie, repeatedly referred to the "alliance"—or "high-profile alliance"—with Israel as a major achievement of the Vorster government.[5] The evidence reviewed later does suggest that South Africa and Israel are close allies. In any event, as Frederick Shiels notes in a discussion of alliances in his book *Tokyo and Washington*, "to limit a discussion . . . to formal alliances, those sanctioned by a treaty in which the parties in effect say 'we are allies', would be to miss out on much of the action of committed nations throughout history."[6] But some may nonetheless wish to reserve the term *alliance* for relationships with formal treaties and commitments for defense assistance, which are not known to exist between Israel and South Africa. In order to avoid ambiguity, this book tries to do without use of the noun *alliance*.

The next chapter reviews some of the milestones in the links between Israel and South Africa until the early 1970s when the relationship entered its highest phase. After the war of October 1973, policymakers in both countries apparently reached similar conclusions, or saw previous conclusions reinforced, about the desirability of closer ties. The circumstances and the major benefits for each side from increased cooperation are considered next, in the third chapter. The evolving ties culminated in the historic visit of Prime Minister John Vorster to Israel in April 1976, when important agreements for cooperation were signed (chapter 4). The extent and nature of commercial, conventional military and nuclear ties are discussed in chapters 5, 6, and 7. The contention of Israel's supporters that it is "unfair" to discuss Israeli–South African ties when everyone else "does it" is assessed after that, in chapter 8.

The ninth chapter considers the role of the South African Jewish community on the domestic scene in South Africa as well as in the relations between Jerusalem and Pretoria. The evidence does not support the familiar assertion of Israeli spokesmen and some writers that the South African Jewish community is a major reason for Israeli–

South African closeness. The last two chapters examine the "strange bedfellows" thesis. The two states, it is evident, share analogous backgrounds, political perceptions, and situations in contemporary history; the relationship seems to be characterized by a degree of empathy, sense of kinship, and solidarity (chapter 10). The eleventh chapter details where and why the two societies are alike, where they differ, and the consequences for subordinate groups.

NOTES

1. James Adams, *The Unnatural Alliance* (London: Quartet Books, 1984). Some sections of the book, especially those dealing with military and nuclear cooperation, are based on information Adams gathered in Israel, South Africa, and other Western countries, where he held private conversations with military officers and intelligence officials. It is readily apparent to the reader that Adams is concerned mainly with fact and does not have any partisan agenda.

Most reviews of *The Unnatural Alliance* found its information credible. (Adams's political analysis, conclusions, and even his title are on considerably shakier ground; there are also occasional inaccuracies.) In the *National Review*, Kathleen Christison, a former political analyst with the CIA, wrote that "Adams's sources are in general numerous and reliable enough to give the book credibility" and that "the accuracy of the picture he draws of the little heralded alliance between these two nations is undeniable" (April 5, 1985). A review in *Resister*, the journal of the Committee on South African War Resistance, finds that "Adams' forte is fact and his book is full of it" (October–November 1984). Another review, by Dennis Herbstein in the *International Herald Tribune*, reported with implicit acceptance Adams's findings about the "extraordinary alliance between these two outcast states" (June 19, 1984). Adams's own newspaper, the *Sunday Times* of London, published a full page report (April 15, 1984). The book did not go unnoticed by the Israeli press. Its major findings were reported, often in detail but without comment either by journalists or officials. (Due to strict censorship, such information cannot originate in the Israeli press, even if an Israeli journalist was the first to discover it. Once the information is made available to an overseas source and published there, the Israeli press may quote without restriction.) It was not until early 1987 that most of what Adams had written three years earlier began to be widely reported in major dailies, for example, the *Washington Post*, February 22, 1987, p. C1 and the *New York Times*, January 29, 1987, p. A1.

2. See for instance Zdenek Cervenka, *The Organisation of African Unity and Its Charter* (New York and Washington: Frederick A. Praeger, 1968).

3. "Black Nobelist Applauds Jews Aid in Anti-Apartheid Struggles" *Jewish Week*, November 30, 1984, p. 8.

4. "Strangers and Brothers: The Unlikely Alliance Between Israel and South Africa," *Sunday Times*, April 15, 1984. Such references are quite common. In a 1984 report on South Africa's military machine, the bureau chief of the *New York Times* in that country referred to Israel as "an ally of South Africa" (September 13, 1984). Similarly, Yoel Marcus, a senior columnist for Israel's leading *Haaretz*, described South Africa—in passing—as "our second most important ally after the United States" (October 1, 1982).

5. Eschel Rhoodie, *The Real Information Scandal* (Pretoria: Orbis, 1983), pp. 110–22.

6. Fredrick Shiels, *Tokyo and Washington* (Lexington, Mass: D.C. Heath & Co., 1980), p. 5.

CHAPTER 2

The Formative Period: A "Strange Nonalliance"

The seeds of the Israeli–South African partnership were arguably planted at least as far back as 1917, when a famous friendship began between General Jan Christian Smuts, head of the Anglophile South African Party, and Chaim Weizmann, President of the British Zionist Federation and later Israel's first president.[1] As a Christian and white South African, Smuts could easily relate to Zionist ideas and aspirations: Europeans settle under the British Empire umbrella in an ancient homeland promised in the Bible; there they make deserts bloom as they bring the blessings of civilization to primitive natives. To Smuts, it all sounded pleasantly familiar. As a member of the Imperial war cabinet and the British war cabinet, he had access to British policy-makers and was in a position to add his own influence in favor of the landmark Balfour Declaration. In the 1917 document, Great Britain made it known that it would view with favor the creation of a Jewish homeland in Palestine, referring to the indigenous population as "non-Jewish communities." In subsequent years Smuts continued to apply his considerable influence to keep the principles of the Balfour Declaration on the agenda of the British government. Upon his death, the South African leader was eulogized by the first Speaker of the Knesset and acting Israeli President, Yosef Sprinzak, as someone who "is written on the map of Israel and in the heart of our nation."[2] Kibbutz Ramat Yochanan is named after the South African statesman.

In South Africa itself, however, relations between Jews and the authorities had been considerably less harmonious, especially in the decades prior to the establishment of the state of Israel. Struggles over immigration restrictions were a regular feature of Jewish life there.

Most noteworthy was a 1930 law popularly known as the "Quota Act" that was introduced by Daniel Malan, then Minister of Interior, Public Health, and Education. It set numerical ceilings on immigration from southern and Eastern Europe and reduced Jewish immigration to a trickle, as Malan later acknowledged had been the intent. The "Aliens Act," which gave an immigration board authority to refuse admission to South Africa for reasons such as "assimilability," followed seven years later. The flow of Jewish refugees from Europe was, according to one source, reduced further to as few as fifty a year, the need to increase the white/black ratio in South Africa notwithstanding.[3]

From the early 1930s when Nazism was on the ascendancy in Germany, through the end of World War II, South Africa was the scene of severe anti-Semitic agitation, much of which focused on "Jewish capitalism" and "Jewish democracy." The Protocols of the Elders of Zion were being freely disseminated and Johannes Strijdom, who succeeded Malan as Prime Minister, spoke of the cancer of "British–Jewish capitalism."[4] In 1937, the platform of the National Party, then in opposition, demanded that the "Jewish question" be tackled by a ban on immigration and by setting numerical quotas on the participation in the South African economy of those Jews already in the country. The party itself was closed to Jews in the Transvaal province.[5] White South Africans were then often warm towards Zionism but considerably less so towards Jews.

The National Party was officially "neutral" during World War II. The activities and sympathies of its leaders, however, suggested otherwise. Future Prime Minister John Vorster was a "general" in the extremist wing of the already militant organization Ossewa Brandwag (O. B.—"Ox-Wagon Guard") whose members wore swastikas and gave the Nazi salute. The organization opposed the Allies' war effort against Nazism and indeed saw Nazism as an ally against Britain. It further opposed parliamentarianism, favored a one party state under a strong leader, and called for racial purity. An account of the wartime period notes that O. B. seemed ready "to effect a putsch at the appropriate moment".[6] Although opposed by the more pragmatic Malan who thought it unwise to put all eggs in the basket of a Nazi victory, "these doctrines (of the O. B.) were not without effect on the political theory of the Afrikanerdom as a whole, which for a while showed a tendency to move gradually in their direction, even in purely Calvinistic circles."[7] Vorster himself would later maintain that he was only anti-British, but in 1942 he explained that: "We stand for Christian Nationalism which is an ally of National Socialism . . . In Italy it is called Fascism, in Germany National Socialism, and in South Africa Christian Nationalism."[8]

John Vorster was interned for twenty months for his activities against the war effort of the Jan Smuts government. After the war Vorster explained, "I am quite satisfied that what I did was right. I was against the war and I campaigned against it. I would do it again."[9]

Dr. Hendrik Verwoerd, Vorster's predecessor as Prime Minister, had a comparable record. In 1936, when he was teaching at the University of Stellenbosch, Verwoerd organized a group of professors to campaign against the admission of Jewish refugees from Germany. As editor of *Die Transvaler*, organ of the National Party, Verwoerd continued this campaign and gleefully reported each Nazi advance.[10]

"Moderate" Daniel Malan accused Jews of "disruptive activities" in trade unions and urged that Jewish immigration be opposed by a "Nordic Front." In 1940 he charged that Smuts was allowing South Africa to become a "Jewish–Imperialistic war machine."[11] In addition, before World War II, Malan reportedly agreed to a German proposal to divide control over Africa between the two countries. This information is said to have been found after the war in German Foreign Ministry documents.[12]

President P. W. Botha was a full-time political organizer for the National Party in Cape Province from 1936 to 1946, a position in which he reportedly used "strong-arm tactics."[13] A great deal can be learned about the past of the man who today heads the South African government from an open letter to him written in 1984 by Donald Woods, the South African political exile and former editor of the *Daily Dispatch*:

How ironic that you visited Britain and France last week during commemoration of the Normandy D-day landings, which insured the Allied victory in World War II—during which conflict you and your colleagues in the Afrikaner Nationalist Party fervently hoped that victory would go to the Third Reich.

Considering how bitterly you attacked Jan Christian Smuts' Government for supporting the Allies at that time, and how openly your party admired Hitler, it was in character when you Afrikaner Nationalists took power in 1948 to pursue your own Herrenvolk theory of apartheid—and today, under your leadership, the cause of racial purity flourishes more strongly than ever before. Since January, more than 50,000 blacks have been arrested under the Pass

Laws, one of your thriving 317 racial statutes that make apartheid first cousin to Hitler's Nuremberg Laws against the Jews.

Speaking of Jews, it is also ironic that your Government is so friendly with Israel, considering that in 1943 you were chief organizer in Cape Province of the party that tried to stop General Smuts' allowing Jewish refugees into South Africa. Not to mention the "Hoggenheimer" cartoons in your party press then—those caricatures of a greedy Jew who was supposedly behind every conspiracy against the Afrikaner Volk. . . . [14]

By an accident of history, the year 1948 marked both the establishment of the Jewish state and the electoral victory of the National Party in South Africa. As the first Prime Minister, Daniel Malan promptly recognized the newly proclaimed state. South Africa was among the world's first countries to do so.[15] Israel was already fighting its first war and the South African government allowed volunteers to join and fight alongside the Israeli army, an exception to the ban on foreign military service by South African citizens. Currency transfers to Israel were also permitted. Several years later, in 1953, Malan was the first head of state to visit Israel.[16] (By comparison, the first British Prime Minister to visit Israel was Margaret Thatcher in May of 1986.)

Little else that would be noteworthy occurred between South Africa and Israel in the 1950s. Trade ties began to develop, primarily the purchase of diamonds for the new industry Israel was developing. At the same time, the Israeli government was on record as opposing apartheid as a matter of principle. In 1952, for instance, Israel voted in favor of establishing a United Nations commission to study the internal policies of South Africa.[17]

Ties between the two countries were set back in the early to mid-1960s. The era of decolonization, which was being followed with concern in South Africa, led to an expansion in the membership of the United Nations and turned the land of apartheid into a "pariah" on the world scene. Beginning with Ghana's independence in 1957, the colonial era was virtually over by 1964. Not only was the South African government under fire from the international community, it also had to cope with continuing and mounting domestic unrest.

At that difficult time for Pretoria, Israel chose black Africa as the focus of its diplomacy. The new African states possessed substantial natural resources and, more importantly, appeared to hold the key to easing Israel's political isolation. Israel had been dealt a rather painful political blow in 1955 when it was excluded from the conference of Afro-Asian, nonaligned countries in Bandung, Indonesia. Israel sought to jump over the fence of international isolation and the Arab boycott. New friends would be particularly welcome in the General Assembly of the United Nations, an arena that was regarded as more important than it is today and where friendly Western countries could not veto troublesome resolutions as they did in the Security Council. Egypt's Gamal Abdel Nasser was also competing for friends and influence in black Africa.

In 1961 Israel voted in favor of the first major United Nations resolution calling for sanctions against South Africa—a resolution opposed by the West—as well as for the motion of censure against Foreign Minister Eric Louw's attempt to defend apartheid before the General Assembly. The November resolution described apartheid as "reprehensible and repugnant to human dignity."[18] Golda Meir, the future Israeli Prime Minister, is said to have pledged not to set foot in South Africa for as long as apartheid existed.

Israel's African policies paid off for most of the decade. African states were reluctant to support anti-Israeli United Nations resolutions. They resisted pressures to unseat Israeli representatives at such forums as the 1962 UN Economic Commission for Africa in Leopoldville and at the 1964 Colloquium on Socialism in Dakar. Israel sent thousands of experts to Africa and trained African students in Israeli universities. Numerous African leaders visited Israel between 1958 and 1965.

As seen through white South African eyes, however, Israel's stance at the United Nations was highly ungrateful as well as hypocritical. After the 1961 votes, Pretoria restricted the transfer of contributions to Israel. White doubts about Jewish loyalty increased, as did anti-Semitic acts, although the South African Jewish press joined the rest of the media in sharply criticizing the Israeli votes. The Afrikaans *Die Transvaler* asked, "Is there any real difference between the way that the people of Israel are trying to maintain themselves amid non-Jewish peoples and the way the Afrikaner is trying to remain what he is? The people of Israel base themselves upon the Old Testament to explain why they do not wish to mix with other people; the Afrikaner does this too."[19]

Prime Minister Hendrik Verwoerd concurred. The Israelis, he noted, took Israel from the Arabs after the Arabs had lived there for a thousand years. In that I agree with them. Israel, like South Africa, is an apartheid state. People are beginning to ask why, if Israel and its rabbis feel impelled to attack the policy of separate development, the policy of separate development in Israel is not wrong in their eyes as well. . . . It may be said that they wish to differentiate in separate states because of religious and not racial differences, but if differentiation is wrong on one score, it is also wrong on another.[20]

But the resentment against Israel was temporary and did not for long preempt its generally favorable image in South Africa. It was not difficult to see that "In the same period, Israel was developing close ties with Black Africa and some circles in her government foolishly believed that this meant taking sides against South Africa."[21]

And similarly, in retrospect,

Several years ago . . . the relationship was not so cordial. Israel then tried to obtain Black Africa's support in the United Nations and a swipe at South Africa was a small price to pay for that support. Today Israel herself is a victim of a prejudiced majority in the UN. She knows what unfounded accusations are like and how a country can be reduced to the pole-cat of the world.[22]

The 1967 war further strengthened pro-Israeli sentiments in South Africa and helped highlight the potential for future cooperation by showing Pretoria the way a Western-oriented country can deal with troublesome Third World neighbors. South African whites felt inspired by the Israeli victory; it was a major psychological boost that proved that highly unfavorable numerical odds could be overcome with superior technology and the proper motivation. The Vorster government relaxed the stringent currency regulations and allowed South African Jews to transfer to Israel $20.5 million to help the war effort.[23] Hundreds of volunteers flew to Israel and some joined military units. Spare aircraft, military equipment, and supplies from the blood bank were also reportedly flown. Attuned to the new political winds, *Die Burger*, organ of the National Party in Cape Province, explained why Israel was worthy of all the assistance:

Israel and South Africa have a common lot. Both are engaged in a struggle for existence and both are in constant clash with decisive majorities in the United Nations. Both are reliable foci of strength within the region which would, without them, fall into anti-Western anarchy. It is in South Africa's interest that Israel be successful in containing her enemies, who are among our own most vicious enemies. . . . The anti-Western powers have driven Israel and South Africa into a community of interests which had better be utilized than denied.[24]

Although Israel still needed black Africa's support, perhaps even more so than before the war, cooperation with South Africa increased markedly. The thaw in relations was evident in increased commercial links, with the growing participation of state-financed corporations. An Israeli-South African Friendship League was founded at the initiative of Knesset Members Eliezer Shostak and Shmuel Tamir in January of 1968. The League was headed by Menachem Begin, whose party supported South Africa on the issue of apartheid because of that country's friendly attitude to Israel and the local Jewish community.[25] The year 1968 saw the establishment of the Israeli–South African Trade Association as well. Shimon Peres, then Secretary-General of the Labor Party, visited South Africa and met with Minister of Defence P. W. Botha.[26] Former Prime Minister David Ben-Gurion and General Chaim Herzog visited the following year; Ben-Gurion met with Prime Minister Vorster.[27] Still, black Africa remained generally friendly. It was not until the early 1970s that Israel's ties with South Africa began to draw attention.

By 1971, as C. L. Sulzberger of the *New York Times* noted after a trip to South Africa, the countries were in a "remarkably close if little known partnership." "The basic truth," he wrote, "remains that this country, which has few friends abroad, regards Israel as one of them," although "for diplomatic reasons, neither overstresses the bond in public" as has always been the case. The article, which gave some "unconfirmable" examples of military cooperation, was titled "Strange Nonalliance."[28]

The relationship was to suffer only one other setback of some significance. In the summer of 1971, Israel offered a token financial contribution to the African Liberation Committee of the Organization of African Unity. In part, this may have been an attempt to reassure black Africa of Israel's interest despite the increasingly visible cooperation with Pretoria. This step was assailed by Menachem Begin, who headed the political opposition. The Israeli Consul-General, I. Unna, asked South Africans to understand: "Israel does not expect

South Africa's blessing for its decision but it does expect South Africans to understand the political and other reasons for its action."[29] Although the contribution was rejected,[30] Pretoria felt betrayed once again and temporarily discontinued the flow of currency to Israel. The setback amounted to little more than a blip on the graph of South African–Israeli relations, however.[31] Even at the height of the dispute, Israeli officials and Knesset members continued to visit South Africa. A delegation of South African Parliamentarians visited the Knesset in October 1971. The following year South Africa opened its first diplomatic mission in Tel Aviv.[32] The coming years were to bring closer and closer ties, and the above blips on the graph would recede into history.

NOTES

1. James Adams, *The Unnatural Alliance* (London: Quartet Books, 1984), p. 4. In the Autumn 1973 issue of the *Journal of Palestine Studies* Richard Stevens provides a much more detailed description of this friendship.

2. Adams, *The Unnatural Alliance*, p. 5.

3. Richard Stevens, "Zionism, South Africa, and Apartheid: The Paradoxical Triangle," *Phylon* 2, (1971).

4. Robert G. Weisbord, "The Dilemma of South African Jewry," *The Journal of Modern African Studies*, 5:2 (1967), p. 235.

5. Sheila Patterson, *The Last Trek: A Study of the Boer People and the Afrikaner Nation* (London: Routledge & Kegan Paul, 1957), p. 290; also *Encyclopaedia Judaica*, (Jerusalem: Keter Publishing House, 1972), 15, col. 190.

6. Michael Roberts and A.E.G. Trollip, *The South African Opposition 1939–1945* (London: Longmans, Green & Co., 1947), p. 192.

7. Ibid.

8. Alexander Hepple, *South Africa: Workers Under Apartheid* (London: Published by Christian Action Publications Ltd. for the International Defence and Aid Fund, 1971), p. 3.

9. *Current Biography Yearbook*, 1967 (New York: The H. W. Wilson Co.), p. 443.

10. *Current Biography Yearbook*, 1959. (New York: The H. W. Wilson Co.), p. 467; also Patterson, *The Last Trek*, p. 290.

11. Patterson, *The Last Trek*, p. 291.

12. *Horizon* (East Germany) cited in *Jewish Affairs* (SA), March 1980, p. 79.

13. *Current Biography Yearbook*, 1979. (New York: The H. W. Wilson Co.), p. 42.

14. *New York Times*, June 10, 1984.

15. Adams, *The Unnatural Alliance*, p. 5. The author says South Africa was "the first" country to recognize Israel, an assertion repeated in the afore-mentioned April 15, 1984 review article in the London *Sunday Times*, as well as in *South African Panorama*, August 1978, p. 9.

16. Naomi Chazan, "The Fallacies of Pragmatism: Israeli Foreign Policy towards South Africa," *African Affairs*, April 1983, p. 172.

17. Rosalyne Ainslee, "Israel and South Africa: An Unlikely Alliance?", United Nations Department of Political and Security Affairs, Centre Against Apartheid, 1981, no. 81-18876. See also *United Nations Official Records*, General Assembly Ad Hoc Political Committee, November 18, 1952.

18. Dusan J. Djanovich, ed., *United Nations Resolutions* (Dobbs Ferry, N.Y.: Oceana Publishers, Series I, 8, 1960–1962), p. 242.

19. Cited by Henry Katzew in "Jews in the Land of Apartheid," *Midstream*, December 1962, p. 73.

20. *Rand Daily Mail*, November 23, 1961.

21. *The Jewish Herald* (SA), April 13, 1976.

22. *Die Oosterlig*, January 13, 1976. Translated in *Jewish Affairs* (South Africa, February 1976).

23. Adams, *The Unnatural Alliance*, p. 13.

24. *Die Burger*, May 29, 1968. Translated in Richard Stevens and A. M. Elmessiri, *Israel and South Africa: The Progression of a Relationship* (New York: New World Press, 1976), p. 196.

25. Michael Brecher, *The Foreign Policy System of Israel* (New Haven: Yale University Press, 1974), p. 173.

26. Ainslee, "Israel and South Africa," p. 6.

27. Ibid.

28. *New York Times*, April 30, 1971.

29. *American Jewish Yearbook* (New York: American Jewish Committee, 1972), p. 586.

30. Chazan, "The Fallacies of Pragmatism," p. 172.

31. The continued development of trade, tourism, and possibly military ties as well is detailed by Joshua David Kreindler in "South Africa, Jewish Palestine and Israel: The Growing Relationship 1919–1974," *Africa Quarterly* (1981) 20:(3–4).

32. After independence Israel established a legation in Pretoria and a Consulate General in Johannesburg, but South Africa chose to be represented through Britain as a member of the Commonwealth. In 1961 South Africa lost its Commonwealth status and with it the representation in Israel.

CHAPTER 3

Digging in After October 1973: Different Problems, Similar Conclusions

In the early to mid 1970s, both Israeli and South African planners were forced to cope with a number of unwelcome political and military challenges to the status quo in their respective regions. Those challenges appear to have underscored to both Jerusalem and Pretoria that the other would be a potentially valuable ally.

The Egyptian and Syrian attacks that began the October 1973 war caught Israel almost completely unprepared. Sadat's troops had little difficulty overrunning the "Bar-Lev" line on the Israeli-held side of the Suez Canal, and the vigorous Syrian offensive on the Golan Heights made similar impressive gains in the first stages of the war. The initial setbacks suffered by the Israeli army, later reversed, led to a political crisis after the war. Much of the earlier confidence that the Israeli army was nearly omnipotent and invincible was lost overnight.

As in 1948 and 1967, during the war, white South Africa's heart was with Israel because, as Defence Minister P. W. Botha noted, "what's happening to them today may happen to us tomorrow."[1] Support was not limited to words of solidarity. Volunteers flew to Israel again. The Finance Ministry relaxed all currency regulations in order to facilitate transfers to Israel. There were even unconfirmed reports of South African military aid; thus it was reported in London that South African pilots flew their jets to the Suez front (using a circuitous route, possibly through Portuguese territories) to get combat experience while assisting the Israelis.[2]

In addition to the traumatic surprise attack, 1973 marked the rise of the Organization of Petroleum Exporting Countries (OPEC) and with it Israeli fears that friendly Western powers could be pressured or influenced ("oil blackmail"). But the worst was yet to come: by the end of the year, all but four black African states severed all official relations with Israel; Mauritius followed in 1976. The other three—Lesotho, Malawi, and Swaziland—are effectively in South Africa's orbit and are considered outside mainstream African politics. The reasons for the break with black Africa, which left Israel isolated as never before, are complex and traceable years before the world heard of "Arab oil power." In the 1950s and 1960s, Israel's voting pattern and sources of support at the United Nations had already set it apart from the emerging Third World and closer to the West.[3] An ally of France, Israel opposed Algerian independence at the UN; it supported secessionist movements in Nigeria and Southern Sudan and was accused of supplying arms to the Portuguese. In the early 1970s, a failed attempt of the Organization of African Unity (OAU) to mediate in the Middle East conflict aroused concern and criticism of Israel, which was seen as intransigent about withdrawal from the occupied territories.[4] For many African leaders, the inviolability of territorial integrity was a serious matter. The chairman of the Committee of Ten, which had attempted the mediation effort, reported at the 1972 OAU summit meeting that "Israel strongly rejected any peace settlement and was even more opposed to anything that might lead to withdrawal of its forces from occupied territories."[5] By 1972 much of Africa already supported the Arab position on the occupied territories, Israeli settlements, and the Palestinians.[6]

The October war highlighted the close ties Israel had with two of black Africa's enemies—Portugal and especially South Africa. Only then did these ties begin to draw attention and became an issue for African states. (The Israeli–South African cooperation was not mentioned in any OAU resolution prior to 1973.[7]) In addition, by 1973 attempts to tighten African and Moslem solidarity made at previous OAU summit meetings and other forums began to bear fruit; oil states made promises of financial support and preferential oil prices. When, in October 1973, Israel briefly occupied Egyptian territory west of the Suez Canal, most of black Africa severed diplomatic relations with it, although informal ties have continued in many cases. Six states severed relations before the October war and the rise of OPEC, and Guinea did so during the June 1967 war. (A few African states have since restored diplomatic relations: Mobutu's Zaire, Liberia, Ivory Coast, Cameroon and Togo. At this writing, it is expected that one or two other African conservative governments will follow suit in the near future.)

In any event, black Africa's break with Israel was seen there as a cowardly betrayal at a time when South Africa acted like a friend in need.[8] With the "loss" of black Africa, the incentive to keep the ties with the white minority regime on the back burner was lost as well. Israel was ready to respond to South Africa's open arms and to do so unapologetically. These sentiments were expressed rather bluntly by Yosef Lapid, a prominent *Maariv* commentator who wrote an article titled "For the Sake of South Africa I Shall Not Keep My Silence," paraphrasing a familiar Jewish pledge about Zion:

After they abandoned us at our most difficult hour . . . we are relieved of the need to be circumspect by which we have abided in the past. . . . The supposedly liberated African states are for the most part a bad joke and an affront to human dignity. . . . All these years I had the feeling we were fooling the public when, for reasons of diplomacy, we did not tell them that most black African states are a nauseating mess. . . .

A few weeks ago Professor Baker's research was published in Britain which, among other things compared the history of Jews and Negroes in New York so as to investigate differences in achievement obtained by races with different IQs and different aptitudes under constant conditions. . . . Evidently, there is, after all, a hereditary difference in intellect between a man whose father lived in the jungle and one whose forefathers were priests in the Temple, as D'Israeli put it. . . .

It is very regrettable that South Africa's white rulers found it impossible to grant the greatest amount of civil rights to the Negro majority in their country. I presume they would have done so if only they could trust that the black majority would not oppress the white minority, would not rob it and would not turn a wealthy and prosperous country into another parody of political independence. . . .

For the life of me, if I have to choose between friendship with today's black Africa and friendship with a white, organized and successful country with a thriving Jewish community, then I prefer South Africa. It is only too bad we waited for the Negroes to throw us out.[9]

Lapid later became head of the Israeli Broadcasting Authority, which oversees state radio and television. How widespread was the preference in Israel for the "white, organized, and successful" country may be impossible to tell. Looking back, however, it seems clear that the political winds in Israel were blowing in Lapid's direction. Israeli leaders were reaching similar conclusions about the short and long-term pay-offs of closer ties with South Africa.

For a country surrounded by enemies and with few friends else-where in the world, the prospect of closer ties with a wealthy and powerful South Africa must have had considerable appeal. Such an ally would not be susceptible to Third World pressures and would be unlikely to exact a political price for supplying Israel with vital re-sources. South Africa's cheap and plentiful coal, for instance, held the promise of meeting some of Israel's energy needs at a time when oil crises and the rising power of OPEC were of great concern. Equally important or perhaps more so might have been South Africa's posses-sion of uranium reserves after a war that eroded confidence in Israel's conventional superiority. In addition, the fate of former United States ally South Vietnam could not have gone unnoticed in Israel, a country greatly dependent on Washington's largesse. This too would under-score the need for military self sufficiency and a reliable partner, or at least a major customer, for the Israel arms industry. In any event, as many Israelis would say, beggars cannot be choosers. The case for closer ties with South Africa—and with Portugal, which at the time was losing its colonies—was articulated by General Chaim Herzog, now President of Israel and always a highly influential political and military analyst. The *Haaretz* article he wrote was titled "Time for Initiatives":

During the war we enjoyed unreserved sympathy in South Africa, which is the strongest power on the African continent. The Arabs are making big noises about an oil embargo against South Africa, Portugal and Rhodesia. But South Africa, with its gold power, can withstand it. . . .

We only have one criterion: Is it good for the Jews or not, and there is no justification for our relations with South Africa or Portugal—the only Euro-pean country which permitted U.S. planes with vital supplies to land on their way to Israel—to be different from their relations with other Western coun-tries. We must develop adequate relations with any country in the world which is willing to have such relations with us. . . . Our geopolitical situation also calls for a fundamental change in our attitude towards a country like South Africa.[10]

And change it did. As Dr. Charles Fincham, the first South African Ambassador to Israel observed,

The turning point in our relations with Israel was undoubtedly the Yom Kippur war and its tragic aftermath. . . . At this time our former Prime Minister and our present Prime Minister, then Minister of Defence, made some public references to Israel's plight. The sympathy implicit in these remarks was not lost on the Israeli press and public opinion. The latent support for South Africa, which we knew existed but which had been difficult to quantify, came to the surface. Why, it was asked, had Israel been supporting resolutions in the United Nations which were hurtful to South Africa when South Africa now stood revealed as one of the few countries to stand up and be counted when Israel was in peril?[11]

As it happened, those were trying times for the prospective South African partners as well. The regime in Rhodesia was on its last legs. The 1974 coup in Portugal was to lead to the end of colonial rule in Angola, to be replaced by an unwelcome radical and hostile government. The same was true in Mozambique after the overthrow of colonial rule. For South African planners, the nightmare of being surrounded and attacked by black states aided by "the Communists" appeared closer to reality than ever before. The need to obtain the arms and technologies that would offset such unfavorable numerical odds seemed urgent.

In fact, quite apart from the political and military realities of the early to mid 1970's, Israel had a role to play in what some South African leaders saw as a strategy for the survival of the republic. In a world in which they are regarded as untouchables, Pretoria's rulers saw the need for a "Total National Strategy," ("TNS") a concept originally developed by P. W. Botha. "TNS" refers to the military, economic, public administration, and foreign policy spheres in which South Africa must mobilize in order to make that part of the world safe for apartheid. The mobilization was made necessary by the "Total Onslaught" against South Africa, the main element of which is the "Communist threat." (The aim of the latter is, as Minister of Defence Magnus Malan pointed out, the "overthrow of the present constitutional order and its replacement by a subject Communist-oriented Black government."[12] That, he warned, is a conspiracy "directed against the whole free Western World.")[13] Regrettably, he continued, most of the Western World either fails to see or is too weak to mobilize against this menace, a theme to which we'll return in the last chapter.

What then can South Africa do to cope with "Marxist expansionism" on the one hand and (at best) Western indifference on the other?

As P. W. Botha explained in an address, there were a handful of foreign policy options, such as for South Africa to attempt to achieve a
regional détente on an anti-Marxist basis, or to become a nonaligned,
neutral country like Switzerland or, as a remote possibility, to make
overtures towards the "Red" enemy. But a more realistic option would
be to "avoid any sort of commitment to any of the major powers and
to seek to develop an alliance with other middle rank powers whose
political philosophies have something in common with ours."[14]

This "pariah option," as it was explicitly called, was to include, in
addition to Israel, such countries as Taiwan, Iran under the Shah, and
Paraguay. Not that prospects for the future appeared particularly bright:
Botha understood that "The shifting fortunes and instability of many
of these states may make this a hazardous enterprise."[15]

Deon Geldenhuys, Assistant Director of the South African Institute
of International Affairs and now Associate Professor of political science at Rand Afrikaans University, concurred that "it does indeed
make sense for the Republic to turn to other friendly pariahs for some
essential goods and services if Western countries are, due to political
considerations, becoming unwilling or unreliable sources of supply."[16] Furthermore, the status of pariah makes it only natural for
such states to collaborate in exploring the nuclear option, Geldenhuys
noted.

In 1974 the Israeli Consulate in South Africa was upgraded to an
embassy, making Israel one of two dozen states—including "homelands"—with diplomatic missions in South Africa.[17] That same year
the Israeli-South African Chamber of Commerce was founded in Tel
Aviv, with a counterpart in Johannesburg. The chambers publish the
Israel-South Africa Trade Journal. In 1975 South Africa reciprocated
the embassy move.

At the United Nations, Israel's voting pattern shifted from condemnation of apartheid to abstention or absence from any vote that had to
do with South Africa. By January 1978, the South African newspaper
The Citizen was able to note that "fourteen new United Nations General Assembly resolutions against apartheid have gone on the books
without the participation of Israel in any of the votes on grounds of
'hypocrisy of Third World sponsors'."[18] The Israeli representatives,
observed one *Haaretz* columnist, would start "looking for the bath-
rooms" whenever a vote on South Africa came up.[19] (Nor had Israel

signed the 1973 United Nations International Convention on the Suppression and Punishment of the Crime of Apartheid). For its part, South Africa has been one of the few countries in the world not to call for Israeli withdrawal from territories occupied in 1967.

High level visits continued. Moshe Dayan visited in 1974 as a guest of the South Africa Foundation and told the South Africans: "I am one of your admirers and I believe you have very many friends," adding that no one could fail to be impressed by the "tremendous civilisation" being created in South Africa. Dayan felt confident that his hosts have "first class troops and good installations in your country and they can take good care of South Africa."[20] South African Minister of the Interior Connie Mulder visited Israel in 1975 and then again in 1976. He met with Prime Minister Izhak Rabin and with the Foreign Minister in preparation for the history-making Vorster visit.[21] The invitation to Vorster was forwared by Defense Minister Shimon Peres who paid a secret visit to South Africa in early 1976.[22] In April of that year, the Israeli Ministry of Trade designated South Africa a "preferred export target." The former "partnership" and "strange nonalliance" was turning into an extensive web of ties, especially in the commercial, military, and nuclear spheres.

NOTES

1. *American Jewish Yearbook*, (New York: American Jewish Committee 1974–1975), p. 557.

2. *Daily Telegraph*, October 31, 1973.

3. This issue is discussed in greater detail in *The Nuclear Axis: Secret Collaboration Between West Germany and South Africa* by Zdenek Cervenka and Barbara Rogers, (New York: Times Books, 1978), pp. 446–47.

4. Olusola Ojo, "Israeli-South African Connections and Afro-Israeli Relations," *International Studies*, January-March 1982, p. 42.

5. Ibid., citing *Africa Research Bulletin*.

6. Ali Mazrui, "Black Africa and the Arabs," *Foreign Affairs*, July 1975, p. 736. Also Ojo, "Israeli-South African Connections."

7. Ojo, "Israeli–South African Connections," p. 47.

8. It is sometimes argued that this is a major reason for South African–Israeli closeness. Naomi Chazan considers the merits of this argument in the aforementioned *African Affairs* article ("The Fallacies of Pragmatism," April 1983) and finds it unconvincing because it fails to explain why "after emotions subsided the South African connection has grown." (p. 194).

9. Yosef Lapid, "Lemaan D'rom Africa Lo Escheshe" ("For the Sake of South Africa I Shall Not Keep My Silence"), *Maariv*, March 14, 1974.

10. Chaim Herzog, "Ha'et Le'iozmot" ("Time for Initiatives"), *Haaretz*, December 7, 1973.

11. Quoted by Willie Breytenbach, "Isolation and Cooperation," *Africa Report*, November-December 1980, p. 41.

12. Deon Geldenhuys, *Some Foreign Policy Implications of South Africa's Total National Strategy* (Braamfontein: South African Institute of International Affairs, 1979), p. 3.

13. Ibid.

14. Ibid.

15. Ibid.

16. Ibid., p. 34.

17. Deon Geldenhuys, *The Diplomacy of Isolation: South African Foreign Policy Making* (New York: St. Martin's Press, 1984), p. 133.

18. *Citizen*, January 17, 1978.

19. Akiva Eldar in *Haaretz*, August 2, 1985. For Israel's voting record on South Africa and apartheid in recent years see Appendix B.

20. *Africa Confidential*, June 20, 1977. Another of Dayan's insights, this time about U.S. blacks, may be relevant here: In a 1980 television interview he said that the United States needed a military draft because "most soldiers are blacks who have a low education and intelligence." A draft, Dayan explained, would result in "better blood and brains." Quoted by Robert Weisbord and Richard Kazarian, *Israel in the Black American Perspective* (Westport, Conn.: Greenwood Press, 1985), p. 160.

21. Rosalynde Ainslee, "Israel and South Africa: An Unlikely Alliance?", United Nations Department of Political and Security Affairs, Centre Against Apartheid, 1981, no. 81-18876, p. 9.

22. Yossi Melman, and Dan Raviv, "Has Congress Doomed Israel's Affair with South Africa?" *Washington Post*, February 22, 1987, p. C2.

CHAPTER 4

Vorster in Jerusalem: Overcoming "A Measure of Unease" About Apartheid

The November 10, 1975, United Nations General Assembly resolution, which stated that Zionism was a form of racism and recalled earlier condemnations of Israel and apartheid, was among the most painful political blows in Israel's history. The resolution was seen there as additional proof that the non-Western world was irredeemably hostile and should be treated as such. "In this age of inflation of statehood," editorialized the *Jerusalem Post* in a typical reaction, "this alliance of weakness and immaturity with cynicism and extortion is sufficient to win a majority in the world organization."[1] In the Knesset, Prime Minister Izhak Rabin compared the resolution to the events of the *Kristallnacht* in Nazi Germany thirty-seven years earlier on the same date. By giving a hand to that "Arab plot," Rabin said, "the UN forfeited any moral and political authority."[2]

The UN no longer seemed to matter. If it previously made sense to downplay the ties with South Africa, that was no longer the case once the international organization appeared "hopelessly lost."[3] Several months later, in April 1976, the world was to witness a spectacular manifestation of South African–Israeli closeness that two or three years earlier would have been unthinkable: a royal reception for Prime Minister John Vorster. "Operation David" was Vorster's third foreign visit in the ten years he had been in office.[4] Former South African Secretary for Information Eschel Rhoodie considered it "South Africa's greatest achievement in international alliance since World War II."[5]

Upon arrival, Vorster was given a red carpet welcome by Prime Minister Rabin and his wife. (According to Deon Geldenhuys of the South African Institute of International Affairs, Rabin had invited him to visit Israel.[6]) As is common for visiting dignitaries, the South African guest, who during World War II spent time in detention for actively opposing the war effort against Nazi Germany, made his first stop in Jerusalem at Yad Vashem, the national shrine for Holocaust victims. Vorster listened to accounts of Nazi crimes, about which he ought to have known a thing or two, and laid a wreath in South Africa's national colors. (Rhoodie recalled that Vorster himself had been very skeptical he would be able to visit Israel given "what was being said" about his past.[7])

The South African Prime Minister also visited kibbutzim, an airforce base, a military aircraft plant, Christian holy sites, factories, and selected areas in the Israeli-occupied territories. He met with Foreign Minister Igal Alon, President Ephraim Katzir, and Teddy Kolek, the mayor of Jerusalem. The South African embassy held a reception at the King David Hotel. Among the guests were Izhak Rabin, Shimon Peres, Igal Alon, Knesset Speaker I. Yeshaiahu, Chief Rabbi Shlomo Goren, Moshe Dayan, Menachem Begin, and Gideon Hausner, the chief prosecutor in Adolf Eichmann's trial.

The apogee of the visit, however, was a state banquet at the Knesset at which Prime Minister Rabin toasted "the ideals shared by Israel and South Africa: the hopes for justice and peaceful coexistence." Both must find ways, Rabin pointed out, "to face up to the problems of dialogue and make coexistence a feasibility in the face of foreign-inspired instability and recklessness."[8] Vorster was so moved he was reportedly unable to speak for a few minutes. Then he noted that "relations with Israel have never been better than now" and assured his Knesset hosts that "I have dedicated myself to work for peace in Africa. There might be temporary setbacks, but in the end I have no doubt that those who desire peace will do their utmost to bring it about."

At the end of his trip, the South African visitor thanked his Israeli hosts and said he felt "at home," without elaborating. One outcome of the trip, officially reported, was a joint ministerial committee that would meet at least once a year to discuss economic, industrial and scientific areas of cooperation. Almost certainly, many additional joint projects that would utilize Israeli know-how and South African resources were discussed. Among them were three additional ports in Israel, an extension of railroad tracks into the Negev desert, and South African assistance in building an oil-and-coal power station between

Haifa and Ashdod.[9] It was also agreed to sharply increase Israeli coal imports from South Africa, perhaps even to strive to make South Africa Israel's exclusive supplier of coal.

The joint ministerial committee was to include the defense ministers; it was during that visit, James Adams wrote in *The Unnatural Alliance*, that a process was set in motion that would ultimately make the two countries a "prime force in the world arms trade."[10] For discussion, see chapter 6.

The significance of Vorster's trip goes well beyond the signing of agreements. The hospitality and ecstatic reactions in both countries are also highly instructive, especially if we try to imagine how Vorster might have been received elsewhere in the world. The leading Israeli journal *Haaretz* saw the trip as a wise and welcome "manifestation of the improving quality of relations between Israel and South Africa." The editorial in the liberal daily noted that much had changed since 1971 when the Israeli Foreign Ministry offered a contribution (to the OAU) that would have reached "anti–South African terrorist organizations." At that time, *Haaretz* went on, Jerusalem sought black Africa's friendship, and apartheid was regarded in Israel as a source of "a measure of unease."[11] *Maariv* described Vorster as a "desirable guest," while *Yediot Aharonot* urged that "the Prime Minister of South Africa ought to be welcomed with the greatest respect we can show. . . ."[12]

Only several dozen leftist demonstrators failed to follow the advice of the *Yediot Aharonot* editorial writer. The opposition, led by Menachem Begin, head of the Israeli–South African Friendship League, warmed up to the visit even more than the official hosts. This near-unanimity did not escape the notice of the South Africans: "Not every statesman who visits Israel is assured of a warm reception from both the government and the opposition" observed South Africa's *Jewish Herald* on April 13, 1976. (Henry Kissinger can no doubt attest to that.) Fleur Villiers, political correspondent of the *Sunday Times* of Johannesburg, similarly noted that "the warmth and quality of his reception in this embattled country since his arrival on Thursday has delighted South Africans in the official party. They described the visit as being of tremendous importance."[13]

Indeed, for South African whites the breakthrough was psychological as much as political. "In a world where we have few friends and even fewer countries likely to be agreeable to a visit of this nature, it is all the more noteworthy that Israel is willing to extend this hospitality,'' wrote the *Rand Daily Mail*.[14] A Johannesburg radio commentary noted that no other country had such far-reaching agreements with South Africa.[15] The *Zionist Record* of South Africa was proud that this was the first time in history when two countries so far apart from each other were to establish a joint cabinet committee, and reiterated that times have changed since ''difficulties arose mainly from tensions at the United Nations when Israeli policies with regard to the emergent Third World embarrassed her good relations with the Republic.''[16] The agreements just reached ''will make South Africa and Israel allies in the true sense of the word'' summed up another South African Jewish publication,[17] while *Die Burger* was convinced that ''the Western world needs a courageous minority to inspire and to mobilise the conviction of a majority. South Africa and Israel have the potential to be the joint spearhead of a turning point.''[18]

In the South African House of Assembly, J. J. Engelbrecht congratulated Prime Minister Vorster on his return and expressed his confidence that ''much good will flow from that for South Africa'' at a time when ''necessary arms are being withheld from us by the United States of America as well as European countries with the exception of a few. . . .''[19]

In the rest of the world, however, the reactions were monumentally different. Holland, a Western country friendly to Israel, expressed concern at the government level and advised Israel that the royal treatment extended to Prime Minister Vorster would complicate the effort to demonstrate that there is no connection between Zionism and racism.[20] The Organization of African Unity, the Arab League, and *Pravda* were even less circumspect. The latter denounced the ''racist-Zionist alliance against the African and Arab liberation movements,''[21] a conclusion shared by the *Ghanaian Times*, which saw the visit as ''an escalation of racist resistance to the African Liberation Movement.''[22]

''Operation David'' indeed made the two countries ''allies in the true sense of the word.'' For Prime Minister Rabin of the Labor Party, Vorster became ''my good friend.''[23] If there was anything left of the earlier ''measure of unease'' about apartheid, it could not readily be discerned.

NOTES

1. *Jerusalem Post*, November 12, 1975.

2. *Divrei Haknesset* (The Knesset Record), Jerusalem, November 11, 1975, 75, p. 314.

3. Mordechai Tomarkin, "Yachasei Israel–Drom Africa Baespaclaria Shel Istrategiat Mediniut Hahutz Shel Israel," (The Israeli–South African Relationship as Reflected in the Looking Glass of Israeli Foreign Policy Strategy"), *Skira Hodshit*: A Monthly Journal for IDF Officers, December 1980.

4. Olusola Ojo, "Israeli–South African Connections and Afro–Israeli Relations," *International Studies*, January-March, 1982, p. 44.

5. Eschel Rhoodie, *The Real Information Scandal* (Pretoria: Orbis, Ltd., 1983), p. 111.

6. Deon Geldenhuys, *The Diplomacy of Isolation: South African Foreign Policy Making* (New York: St. Martin's Press, 1984), p. 116. Additional details about the reception can be found in *South African Digest*, April 16, 1976; Benjamin Beit-Hallahmi, "South Africa and Israel's Strategy of Survival," *New Outlook: Middle East Monthly*, April 1977.

7. Rhoodie, *The Real Information Scandal*, p. 112.

8. *South African Digest*, April 16, 1976; Beit-Hallahmi, "South Africa and Israel's Strategy."

9. James Adams, *The Unnatural Alliance* (London: Quartet Books, 1984), p. 17. The text of the agreement has not been made public.

10. Ibid., p. 74.

11. "Oreach Midrom Africa" ("A Guest from South Africa"), *Haaretz*, April 6, 1976.

12. *South African Panorama*, June 1976.

13. *Sunday Times*, April 11, 1976.

14. *The Rand Daily Mail*, cited in the *Zionist Record* (South Africa, April 14, 1976).

15. Ojo, "Israeli–South African Connections," p. 47.

16. *Zionist Record* (South Africa, April 14, 1976).

17. *Jewish Herald* (South Africa, April 20, 1976).

18. Dawie in *Die Burger*, cited in *South African Digest*, April 30, 1976.

19. *South African House of Assembly Debates*, Cape Town, April 21, 1976, pp. 5091–92.

20. *New York Times*, April 18, 1976.

21. Ibid.

22. Cited by Ojo, "Israeli–South African Connections," p. 48.

23. Major Gerald Keller (USMC), "Israeli–South African Trade: An Analysis of Recent Developments," *Naval War College Review*, Spring 1978, p. 74, citing *Africa Report*.

CHAPTER 5

Economic Ties: "We Can Really Go Places If We Join Forces"

The South African–Israeli relationship is not about trade, at least not in the conventional, civilian sense of the term. Nonetheless, at least until early 1987 when this relationship received some front page coverage in the Western press, Israeli–South African ties often used to be associated with "trade," even in the minds of those who might have been expected to know better.[1] The mistaken focus on trade has been an easy target for Israeli spokesmen and supporters, who would triumphantly point to the considerably larger trade some other countries had with Pretoria and sometimes proceed to talk about double standards and anti-Semitism.

What is the extent of Israeli–South African trade? Depending on what is included in the computation, the amount of trade can be made to look ridiculously small—as the Israeli Consulate and the Anti-Defamation League are likely to argue—or in league with South Africa's larger trading partners in the West. Not all of this is willful misrepresentation, although that does seem to be a factor.

The International Monetary Fund reports world import and export data. According to these data, Israel imports from South Africa materials such as steel, coal, timber, and sugar; South Africa's imports from Israel include fertilizers, pharmaceuticals, textiles, and machinery. The annual *Direction of Trade Statistics* also indicates that these imports and exports are relatively miniscule in relation to each country's total trade. Thus South Africa exported to the United States $2.2 billion worth of goods in 1980, and $1.5 billion in 1983. It imported $2.5 billion worth of American goods in 1980, and $2.2 billion in 1983. For South Africa and Japan, the above figures were $1.5, $1.4,

$1.6,and $1.7 billion, respectively. However the declared trade with Israel for the same years was $95, $142, $26, and $61 million, respectively.

Proportionately, in the early 1980s trade with Israel represented less than half a percent of South Africa's total imports and 0.7 percent of its exports; as a proportion of Israel's total trade, the figures were about 1 and 2 percent, respectively.[2] Despite a tenfold expansion in the 1970s alone,[3] South African–Israeli trade continues to appear humble even by comparison with Pretoria's trade with (all of) black Africa, which is another favorite argument of Israeli diplomats in the West.

The most recent civilian trade figures available at this writing show that in the first eleven months of 1986 Israel's imports from South Africa reached $144 million, and its exports there reached $41 million. The comparable figures for 1985 were $175 and $64 million.[4] The weakness of the South African rand in recent years has had a detrimental effect on the profitability, and hence the amount, of Israeli civilian exports to South Africa. (For instance, in the early 1980s, numerous socialist kibbutzim found in South Africa a major market for their agricultural products and equipment; exports were worth $8 million a year. By 1987, these exports were down to $3 million.[5])

But in the real world, there is much more to the category of trade in Israeli–South African relations than the civilian items that the two countries choose to report. We are no longer dealing with precise figures, and estimates can vary greatly, but that is probably not too high a price to pay for being closer to the truth. For instance, James Adams, the author of *The Unnatural Alliance*, corrected for the absence of diamonds and military transfers from official figures and went as far as to argue, "while it is impossible to place an accurate figure on the true total volume, it is probable that when all trade is taken into account, Israel may be South Africa's biggest trading partner."[6]

Wildly varying estimates of South African–Israeli "trade" are nothing new. Even those officials who are directly involved in commercial relations do not always seem to be in agreement. A 1979 *Financial Mail* (South Africa) special supplement dealing with the economic ties with Israel quoted Ephraim Raviv, Economic and Commercial Counselor at the Israeli embassy in Pretoria and director of the Israeli Trade and Tourism Center in South Africa:

The volume of trade between Israel and South Africa is still small and disappointing and its importance should not be exaggerated. Figures have certainly grown in absolute terms but we have a long way to go before we can say we're satisfied. The export/import trade with South Africa amounts to less than 1% of Israel's total trade.

But the report also quoted Dr. Jacques Baranes, chairman of the Israeli–South African Chamber of Commerce and senior manager of Israel Discount Bank: "Until a few years ago we used to trade in figures of $15m-$20m, a fraction of each country's $10 billion-$12 billion trade with the world. But we are now dealing in hundreds of millions of dollars. We have a real and important trade partnership." [7]

The *Financial Mail* report noted that the contradiction could be easily reconciled if diamonds, which are bought in London, are taken into account. The value of this import item was $1 billion in 1978, which in itself was more than a sixfold increase since the beginning of the decade. For Israel—whose Ministry of Trade had designated South Africa a "preferred export target" in 1976[8]—the apparent trade imbalance would have been worrisome, but in fact "hardly anyone [in Israel] appeared overly worried about the imbalance in trade in favour of South Africa," the *Financial Mail* report continued, due to the "undisclosed trade items—on the value of which nobody is prepared to venture even an anonymous guess. One thing is certain: South Africa is a highly valued client of Israel's electronics industry."

It was not until early 1987 that informed estimates of the value of Israeli–South African military trade were published in the Israeli and American press. In 1986 Israel probably earned between $400 and $800 million from the military equipment and know-how it exported to South Africa.[9]

Turning to diamonds, this Israeli industry is currently estimated to generate earnings of $1 billion a year. Its sales and fortunes have fluctuated, as have the figures cited by various sources. The above 1979 *Financial Mail* trade supplement reported that the previous year Israel had imported in excess of $1 billion worth of diamonds for its industry "and the bulk of them originate in South Africa." [10] Yet today Israel buys diamonds from several sources, and it is all but impossible to tell just how much comes directly from South Africa. South Africa is no longer a dominant player in the diamond trade, although in the popular mind it continues to be associated with diamonds. The Central Selling

Organization in London is a subsidiary of DeBeers, the South African mining concern, but only a fraction of the diamonds it sells originate in South Africa. The remainder come from other countries in Africa as well as from the Soviet Union and Australia.

With or without diamonds, for an economy the size of Israel's the share of trade with Pretoria must rank among the world's highest.

At the root of Israeli–South African commercial links there has always been a marriage of needs. For a country such as Israel, the ideal ally would be powerful, rich in natural resources (for example, cheaply-mined coal, which in 1985 supplied 65 percent of Israel's needs[11]) and also, as the London *Economist* observed, such an ally "should not be too susceptible to American influence; should have shared geopolitical interests with Israel; and above all should have the resources and technology to help build a sophisticated weapons industry. South Africa seemed to fit the bill." [12]

For South Africa, the Israeli connection has meant a golden opportunity to gain back-door access to Western markets. Israel enjoys duty-free access to the European Economic Community (EEC) as well as to the United States under the Generalized System of Preferences. The agreements do not require that a product marked "made in Israel" be manufactured there in its entirety: a 40 percent Israeli-added value can qualify. Further, Israel has a large number of export-oriented industries, and transportation costs to Europe and the United States, its main export markets, are lower than those from South Africa. It did not take long for Israeli and South African officials and businessmen to recognize the opportunities.

The offer to use Israel as a stepping-stone to Western markets—a "vital bridgehead for South African exports"—in the words of Israeli expert Naomi Chazan,[13] was made by Israeli Finance Minister Simcha Erlich, who visited South Africa in February 1978 heading an economic delegation.[14] This Israeli readiness to serve as trans-shipment station has recently been looked up to as a potential lifeline for South Africa in case Western sanctions become tighter. In early 1985, in the midst of Israeli-American trade negotiations, Director-General of the South African Department of Finance Dr. Joop de Loor pointed to "quite a number of opportunities" becoming available to South African manufacturers for "triangular export." He was speaking at a Johannesburg luncheon sponsored by the South Africa–Israel Chamber of Commerce.[15] These opportunities have also been dissected in a

University of Cape Town MBA thesis with the forward title "A Study of Some of the Factors Influencing the Use of Israel as a Springboard for South African Exports."[16]

A number of joint ventures have been established in order to take advantage of all that Israel and South Africa can offer each other in the commercial sphere. Speaking at the opening of an Israeli industrial trade fair, T. F. van der Walt, the South African Secretary of Commerce and Consumer Affairs, explained their significance:

Israel could play a significant role in complementing South Africa's economy . . . South Africa has abundant raw materials and labour resources. It has substantial resources of capital of its own and a diversified economic structure. But despite these positive factors we still experience a relative shortage of risk capital and technical skills. In this particular field, a country like Israel could also play a significant role in harnessing these extensive raw material resources in the form of joint ventures to the benefit of both countries.[17]

The Secretary's thoughts echoed those of former Israeli Consul General I. Unna, who was not content with merely trading with South Africa: "With South Africa's abundance of raw materials and Israel's know-how we can really go places if we join forces."[18]

The most important joint venture is Iskoor, established in Israel by the South African Iron and Steel Corporation (ISCOR) and the Koor concern, which is controlled by Israel's labor federation, the Histadrut. (The Histadrut has adopted an antiapartheid public stance and has maintained contacts with South African black labor leaders.) The labor federation is a major factor in the Israeli economy since it is both the country's chief trade union and the largest nongovernmental employer; one out of every four Israeli workers is employed by the Histadrut. Iskoor was established in order to process and distribute South African steel. Already in 1977 *The Star* in South Africa reported in the October 7 business section that "Israel is fast emerging as a springboard for South African steel to the EEC and the United States." The report was confirmed by Dr. Tamir Agmon, professor of finance at Tel Aviv University who came to South Africa as a member of an Israeli economic delegation. The Israelis sought "to encourage local businessmen to use the Israeli connection to enter markets abroad."

Quite a few South Africans were convinced. A May 4, 1979, *Financial Mail* (South Africa) article titled "The Manna Falls" quoted

Archie Hendler of Hendler and Hendler who explained that "the main reason for going into Israel is to gain access to the Common Market." The same was true of the joint venture between Chemtra and the Israeli company Polichrom: "In the long term we are interested in establishing a marketing office which will be used as a springboard to get South African products into Europe." And the chairman of Elron, another Israeli company in a joint venture, agreed that "joint ventures in the semi-processed aluminum field make good sense" since, after all, "we buy most of our semi-processed aluminum from Canada now, we might as well buy it from South Africa."[19] An accord to avoid double taxation was signed in 1978.

In her *African Affairs* article, Naomi Chazan reviewed some of the other civilian joint projects and investments: South African investors, encouraged by favorable terms from both governments, have "poured money into a variety of Israeli schemes, ranging from a new hydroelectric system that will divert water from the Mediterranean to the Dead Sea, regional development projects in the Negev, a plan for linking Eilat and Tel Aviv by rail . . . and a brush factory on a kibbutz."[20] (Not all of these schemes materialized or were successful; the shelving of the hydroelectric project was described in South Africa as a "blow to South African contractors."[21]) South African companies such as Tagun Rubber, a Calan subsidiary, and Transvaal Mattress also operate in Israel.[22] Zim, the sea-freight company, combined with Unicorn of South Africa to form Zimcorn.[23] New projects were regularly considered in the 1970s and early 1980s; in that period visits by officials were "too numerous to mention."[24] By the mid-1980s, 35 percent of non-U.S. foreign investment in Israel came from South Africa.[25]

It is not clear that such joint ventures, with or without "triangular exports," are now major factors in either the Israeli or South African economies. We do know that both Israeli and South African officials have desired and encouraged such an outcome; and, the existing arrangement did not escape the attention of the U.S. Secretary of State's Advisory Committee on South Africa, a twelve member panel that had been appointed in 1985 to analyze and recommend U.S. policies towards that country. In its report, released in mid-February 1987, the commission pointed out that South Africa has in fact benefited from shipping goods to the United States and Europe duty-free after processing and packaging in Israel. (It also called on the Reagan Administration "to prevent countries such as Israel that import U.S. arms and defense material from transshipping such goods to South Africa and selling South Africa technology and material critical to its efforts to attain military self-sufficiency.'')[26]

HOMELANDS

As with joint ventures, Israel is one of very few countries with ties and investments in the South African Bantustans, now officially known as "national states." As early as 1976, Knesset Member Mordechai Ben-Porat said in South Africa that Israel was willing to help develop Transkei.[27] According to later reports, Israeli companies were interested in utilizing "the low-cost semi-skilled labour available in the Republic and then import the goods back to Israel . . . (from where they can be) exported elsewhere, possibly to the EEC."[28]

Although the Israeli government has never recognized the homelands—no government except Pretoria has—the state-owned Agridev agricultural development company has carried out development projects in Ciskei. The Israeli Discount Bank helped finance some of these projects.[29] In 1983 the entire 34-member Venda Chamber of Commerce visited Israel with the encouragement and assistance of the Israel–South Africa Chamber of Commerce.

Israeli telephone directories, which are distributed by the Bezek government-owned company, list Bophuthatswana, Ciskei and Transkei among the "countries" where direct-dialing service is available.

At least two homelands, Ciskei and Bophuthatswana, have been privately represented in Israel. Shabtai Kalmanowitz, a businessman with extensive political connections, has represented Bophuthatswana. Ciskei was represented by two other businessmen, Yosef Schneider and Nat Rosenwasser. They headed the "Ciskei Commercial Delegation" until the summer of 1985, when their contract was terminated in connection with a corruption scandal that was too much even for the rulers of Ciskei. The Nordau Boulevard building where their Tel Aviv office was located sported the Ciskeian flag; they said they were employees of that homeland's Foreign Ministry and the office telephone was answered "Hello, [this is] Ciskei."[30]

Ciskei is in many ways an investor's paradise with low labor costs, low rents, and cheap loans. The authorities have assumed responsibility for as much as 95 percent of the salary of local workers, up to about $50 a month. At the opening ceremony of one of the factories, Chief Lennox Sebe hailed the "Israelis who have faith in the capability of Ciskei to honour its promises and it demonstrates the willingness of our friends from Israel to invest permanently in Ciskei."[31] According to another 1984 *Jerusalem Post* report, ten Israeli-owned factories had been completed or were being built in Ciskei. Among the investors were former Finance Minister (now Knesset Member) Yoram Aridor, reserve brigadier-general Ephraim Poran—a former military adviser to Prime Ministers Rabin and Begin—and other members of the Knesset.[32] The report goes on to describe the human rights record of "President-for-life Sebe [who] has imposed a reign of terror on his people that has left even his apartheid mentors aghast."

The Israeli press provides more details about the activities of Israeli entrepreneurs in the homelands in the mid-1980s. An Israeli businessman is running the Sun hotels and casinos in Sun City, a "mini-Las Vegas" in Bophuthatswana. Business is as good as can be because "gambling, games of fortune, and striptease are banned in South Africa proper." (Israeli guards ensure that things do not get out of hand.) Another Israeli made a fortune by building a factory for "grade-B clothing for black consumers in Venda." Five hundred blacks are working in his factory, most of whose financing came from the Bantustan authorities.[33] Kibbutz Lochamei Hagetaot has, established after World War II by Ghetto and resistance fighters, set up an electronics factory in KwaZulu.

The web of ties with the homelands enabled President Sebe to explain in Israel in 1983, "For the sake of diplomacy, and speaking in parables, I would say that it is an ad-hoc recognition."[34] The occasion was an international tourism exhibition in Tel Aviv. During two other trips to Israel that year, he negotiated the purchase of aircraft and training for eighteen pilots in Israel—presumably the nucleus of a future Ciskeian air force.[35] Counterinsurgency is about the only possible use for such an airforce; the homeland has no international borders to defend and what threat the authorities may face would be from their own population. Lennox Sebe's former security adviser disclosed in an interview with *The Star* (Johannesburg) that in 1982 he and Sebe went to Israel to shop for arms.[36]

Given all this brisk business, ranging from tourism all the way to security, it was not surprising to see the term "homelands lobby" applied to Israeli interests in the Bantustans.[37] The "lobby" included members of the political and military establishments, not merely anonymous entrepreneurs unconnected with the state. James Adams summed up that Israel had "invested millions of dollars in the homelands and its support has done much to underpin the homelands both economically and politically."[38]

But this Bantustan business does little to help Israel in its search for friends and influence in Africa and elsewhere, which is why the accompanying publicity has never pleased Israeli Foreign Ministry officials.[39] In one instance Israeli Minister of Tourism Sharir invited Sebe to a state banquet, but Foreign Ministry officials considered it going too far and attempted to cancel the event. It was too late to cancel, however, so the banquet had to be labeled "unofficial."[40]

Clearly, what is commonly referred to as "trade" between South Africa and Israel is in fact a diversified economic relationship with the potential to serve as a lifeline for Pretoria in the event that Western sanctions become tighter than they are now. If there is opposition and criticism abroad, it is not South Africa's or Israel's problem: As an editorial in the *Israel–South Africa Trade Journal* pointed out, the two countries seem to have adopted the attitude that "the dogs may bark but the trading caravans must go on."[41]

NOTES

1. For instance, at a New York City forum for mayoral candidates, one of the questions had to do with their approach to, of all things, the problem of "Israeli trade" with South Africa. *New York Times*, December 16, 1984, p. 6E.

2. The International Monetary Fund, *Direction of Trade Statistics* (Washington, D.C.: July, 1982), in James Adams, *The Unnatural Alliance* (London: Quartet Books, 1984), p. 19.

3. Naomi Chazan, "The Fallacies of Pragmatism: Israeli Foreign Policy towards South Africa," *African Affairs*, April 1983, p. 179.

4. Yonathan Sherman, "Drom Africa—Haheshbon Hakalkali," ("South Africa—the Economic Calculus"), *Haaretz*, March 20, 1987. In a January 29, 1987 *New York Times* report Thomas Friedman quoted different figures for 1985.

5. Sherman, "Drom Africa".

6. Adams, *The Unnatural Alliance*, p. 19.

7. "The SA Connection," in "Special Report: Israel," Supplement to the *Financial Mail*, September 14, 1979, p. 17.

8. Rosalynde Ainslee, "Israel and South Africa: An Unlikely Alliance?" United Nations Department of Political and Security Affairs, Centre Against Apartheid, 1981, p. 10.

9. *New York Times*, March 19, 1987, p. A12. For a 1985 attempt to reach an estimate of Israeli–South African trade that would take into account what others tended to overlook see Jane Hunter, "Trade with South Africa—How Much?," *Israeli Foreign Affairs* (United States, June 1985), p. 3.

10. "The SA Connection," p. 17.

11. *Journal of Commerce*, July 1, 1985. In an effort to diversify the sources of coal supplies, Israel considered signing a contract with Colombia in the spring of 1987. China and Poland have also been mentioned as possible sources of coal in the future.

12. *Economist*, November 5, 1977, p. 9.

13. Chazan, "The Fallacies of Pragmatism," p. 180. Naomi Chazan has repeatedly criticized what she considers a shortsighted Israeli policy toward South Africa. This *African Affairs* article attempts to show that "Israel has become embroiled in an unequal relationship" whose scope is "meagre" and which benefits mainly "the other partner." Reliable reports on this relationship that became available in early 1987 (for example, in the *New York Times*, January 29 and March 19; the *Washington Post*, February 22 and numerous others) easily refute the above wishful thinking. The relationship is neither "meagre" nor that "unequal" nor does it benefit mostly South Africa.

14. *Haaretz*, February 7, 1978; *Africa Report*, March-April 1978; *Washington Post*, February 8, 1978.

15. *Rand Daily Mail*, February 13, 1985 in *Jewish Affairs* (South Africa, March 1985), p. 87.

16. Z. Shapiro, "A Study of Some of the Factors Influencing the Use of Israel as a Springboard for South African Exports: A Technical Report," University of Cape Town Graduate School of Business, Cape Town, 1979.

17. *The Citizen*, March 18, 1980, in *Jewish Affairs*, April 1980, p. 71. In 1976 the Israeli Trade Consul in South Africa was even more forward: South Africa, he pointed out, was "rich in cheap labour, which Israel lacks," apparently ignoring Gaza and the West Bank, where wages are well under half their level in pre-1967 Israel. *Star* Weekly Edition, April 24, 1976.

18. *Financial Mail*, June 7, 1974.

19. *Financial Mail*, September 14, 1979.

20. Chazan, "The Fallacies of Pragmatism," p. 179.

21. *Financial Mail*, May 11, 1984. The South African business journal published a fifty page supplement on Israel and trade opportunities with it.

22. Chazan, "The Fallacies of Pragmatism," p. 179.

23. *Financial Mail*, May 11, 1984.

24. Benjamin Beit-Hallahmi, "Israel and South Africa 1977–1982: Busi-

ness as Usual—and More," *New Outlook: Middle East Monthly*, February 1983, p. 32.

25. Jane Hunter, "Israel and South Africa: How Close?," *Israeli Foreign Affairs* (United States, February 1985), citing *South African Digest*.

26. *Los Angeles Times*, February 12, 1987; *Haaretz* weekly overseas edition, February 13, 1987.

27. Ainslee, "Israel and South Africa," p. 23.

28. Ibid., p. 24.

29. *Jerusalem Post*, June 20, 1984, p. 1.

30. Shmuel Segev, "Israel Umedinot Hehasut" ("Israel and the Homelands"), *Maariv*, December 2, 1983; *Maariv* weekly overseas edition, April 11, 1985, p. 6.

31. *Jerusalem Post*, July 27, 1984.

32. Roy Isacowitz, "Twinning with a Tyrant," *Jerusalem Post Magazine*, November 9, 1984.

33. Yehoshua Bitzur, "Chavrei Haknesset Gilu et Ciskei" ("Knesset Members Discover Ciskei"), *Maariv*, April 19, 1985. For additional details on investments and high-level visits, see Arieh Lavi, "Kol Anshei Ciskei" ("All the Ciskei Men"), *Haaretz*, June 28, 1985; *Jerusalem Post*, June 20, 1984, p. 1.

34. Adams, *The Unnatural Alliance*, p. 28.

35. *The Citizen*, November 12, 1983, in *Jewish Affairs* (SA), December 1983.

36. Reported by Isacowitz, "Twinning with a Tyrant."

37. *Africa News*, April 2, 1984, citing the *Jerusalem Post*.

38. Adams, *The Unnatural Alliance*, p. 27.

39. Segev, "Israel and the Homelands." For more details on Israel and the Bantustans see Benjamin Beit-Hallahmi's *The Israeli Connection: Who Israel Arms and Why* (New York: Pantheon, 1987), pp. 140–45.

40. Segev, "Israel and the Homelands."

41. Shapiro, "A Study of Some of the Factors Influencing the Use of Israel," p. 9.

CHAPTER 6

Military Affairs: Counterinsurgency, Electronics, and Hardware

South Africa's military strategy has been developed with the help of Israeli officers, her armed forces are equipped by Israel, and their counterinsurgency tactics have evolved almost entirely as a result of the lessons learned by the Israelis in their fight against the Palestine Liberation Organization.[1]

It has been difficult, in the past decade, to find many reports dealing with South Africa's military machine in which the Israeli contribution did not figure prominently. Still, until early 1987 Israeli spokesmen and supporters in the West dismissed evidence of a nearly symbiotic Israeli–South African military relationship as "rumors" and "PLO propaganda." Then, days before April 1 when the Reagan Administration submitted to Congress a report detailing just such government-to-government ties, the Israeli government announced that it would not sign new military contracts with Pretoria—in the future. The existing ones will evidently do nicely.

Even before the report to Congress, preceded by detailed reports in the *New York Times*, *Washington Post* and elsewhere,[2] the details of this relationship were readily available to those who cared to look. But, at least in the American mass media, not many reporters chose to look. In 1984 James Adams observed in *The Unnatural Alliance*, "What is perhaps most surprising about the development of their respective armed forces is that it has all taken place without the world either knowing or caring."[3]

Every Israeli Defense Minister since the 1970s, as well as scores of

Israeli senior officers and intelligence officials, are known to have visited South Africa. The stated purpose of some of the trips was fundraising or other contacts with the Jewish community, but this did not keep the Israeli visitors from meeting with their South African counterparts and discussing arms sales and other cooperation, as was often the case. Among them are generals Meir Amit, Aharon Yariv, Ezer Weizmann, Chaim Bar-Lev, Chaim Herzog, Nathan Nir, Amos Horev (former Chief Scientist of the Defense Ministry), Mordechai Gur, and Izhak Rabin. Ariel Sharon spent ten days in the war zone in Namibia in 1981. Among the South African commanders known to have visited Israel are Major General Neil Webster and Hendrik van den Berghe, chief of the Bureau of State Security.

The South African military has had to live with an international arms embargo since 1963. At first the embargo was voluntary, but when it became a farce due to its many loopholes and weaknesses, Third World countries began to seek stricter provisions. Calls for a more serious embargo were resisted by the West until December 1977, after the Soweto killings the previous year, the death of Steve Biko in police custody, and evidence of South African preparations for a nuclear test (chapter 7). At that time Security Council Resolution 418 determined that the acquisition of arms by South Africa constituted a threat to international security. Hence all members of the United Nations were obligated to stop the supply of weapons, ammunition, and equipment to Pretoria. The granting of new licenses to manufacture such items in South Africa was prohibited; existing licenses were to be reviewed with an eye to terminating them.

No one has ever argued that the embargo was a success, either in its voluntary or "mandatory" versions. Italy, Spain, Israel, and France only begin a rather long list of countries reported to have breached it in one way or another. In part this is because where there is a will, an ambiguity or a loophole can always be found[4]: Even the stricter 1977 resolution fails to define "arms and related materiel" which are supposed to be withheld from South Africa; subsidiaries of Western companies can continue to manufacture arms and equipment inside South Africa; the embargo resolution calls for "reviewing" but does not demand the termination of existing contracts. And then, there is the "dual use" equipment that can be plausibly described as civilian but is in fact used by the army and police.

Even more importantly, little was done or could be about the transfer to South Africa of arms technology, an area in which a country such as Israel has much to offer. Once the know-how is available to South African manufacturers, they can manufacture the hardware locally and even export it later on claiming "self sufficiency." (A modern howitzer, discussed later, is a case in point.) Technology transfers, which save the South African government vast amounts it would otherwise have to spend on independent research and development, can also help save existing weapons such as aging tanks and jet fighters from obsolescence.

Most of South Africa's arsenal is of Western European and American origin. Long regarded as a "strategic asset" for the West because of its minerals and the Cape route, South Africa has been rewarded with massive supplies of weapons from these powers. Britain was the main supplier in the 1950s. In the 1960s and until the mid-1970s, France distinguished itself by shipping to South Africa almost every imaginable kind of conventional weapon—from armored cars to planes and submarines—all this while formally observing the voluntary arms embargo. But France has had interests in the Third World as well, especially in black Africa, and as political scientist Andrew Pierre noted in *The Global Politics of Arms Sales*, by the late 1970 things were no longer the same: "In the second half of the 1970's, as unfavorable Third World opinion led France to curtail its assistance, Israel, another pariah state, emerged as an important arms ally. . . . There can be little doubt that the defense ties with Israel are deep and of growing importance."[5]

Within days after the 1977 embargo resolution, Moshe Dayan said that South Africa was a "good friend" and that Israel would not "leave her to the mercy of fate."[6] After the critical reactions which followed, however, the Israeli government—and Dayan himself—announced that Israel would abide by the embargo. Abide, that is, subject to Israeli reading of the document and certainly excluding commitments made before the United Nations resolution. The net result has been a major Israeli contribution to South African power.

Today South Africa, armed to its teeth, is by far stronger than any combination of neighboring countries. It claims to be the largest arms producer in the Southern hemisphere and to be self-sufficient in many types of light weapons, ammunition, armored vehicles, land mines, and artillery guns. Some of these are available for export. In a 1982 interview, Piet Marais, the head of Armaments Corporation of South

Africa (ARMSCOR) credited the UN embargo with spurring the South African arms industry. He acknowledged that ARMSCOR cooperated with Israel on military technologies, though he played it down. In addition, Marais confirmed reports that South Africa hoped to sell weapons to some countries that do not wish to make the purchase openly—by routing the shipments through Israel and Taiwan.[7]

In 1948, during Israel's first war, more than 1000 volunteers came from South Africa to help the war effort. According to South African Brigadier Jack Penn, that was a higher number than from the United States or Britain.[8] Between the 1948 and 1967 wars, relations between Pretoria and Jerusalem were low-key, as were the military ties. Only insubstantial exchanges of materiel took place. The Israeli Uzi sub-machine gun has been manufactured in South Africa since the early 1960s—under Belgian license. In May 1967, when Egypt's Nasser closed the Tiran straits, South Africa was the first country to offer ships to break the blockade, a former Knesset member wrote.[9] Then, when the war broke out, Israel received aircraft and spare parts from South Africa; in return, Defense Minister Moshe Dayan was asked, and agreed, that Israel would not "bark against South Africa louder than the rest of the pack" at the United Nations. It also agreed to advise the South African forces on "Russian equipment, etc".[10]

The spectacular Israeli victory in that war marked the beginning of increasingly close and systematic ties between the two countries. The South Africans felt particularly inspired by the performance of the besieged few who defeated the many. A triumph of superior technology and training was clearly something to learn from. Indeed, the regular exchange of information and expertise between South Africa and Israel began shortly after the war. A South African military delegation came to Israel to study the war and Mordechai Hod, commander of the Israeli air force, lectured before the South African staff college in October 1967.[11]

The contacts burgeoned in later years, as was confirmed in 1975 by General Meir Amit, former chief of the Israeli secret services and president of Koor industries. Amit, who was in South Africa on a business and lecture tour, said that Israeli officers regularly lectured before their South African counterparts about modern warfare and counterinsurgency, an area in which no other country could provide better advice. When an interviewer pointed out that, in addition to major industrial projects, Israel and South Africa shared good military relations, the Israeli general replied that "that is an understatement."[12]

Shortly after John Vorster's 1976 visit, Israeli officers were reported to be "closely involved" in planning the South African raid against Angola. General R.H.D. Rogers of the SAAF attributed the invaders' low casualties to Israeli evacuation techniques.[13] (On November 5, 1977, the *Economist* reported that two years earlier U.S. Secretary of State Henry Kissinger had secretly asked the Israeli government to send instructors and equipment to assist the South African war against Angola.)

In recent years, hundreds of Israeli instructors have reportedly been attached to South African army units. In the September 19, 1981 issue the *Economist* estimated that two hundred Israeli officers were teaching the South Africans "anti-terrorist tactics." Senior Israeli officers later told James Adams that nearly *three* hundred Israeli advisers were assisting all branches of the South African military. They were training air force and navy personnel, conducting joint weapons research, helping seal the borders against guerillas and sharing counterinsurgency intelligence. Similar training has apparently been provided to hundreds of South Africans inside Israel. (The contacts Israeli officers make in the process are often valuable later on for those who become arms dealers when they retire.) The presence of Israeli advisers in South Africa was raised in the Knesset by K. M. Marcia Friedman but the Defense Ministry denied it.[14]

Quite apart from this government-to-government cooperation, many of the estimated 25,000 Israeli emigrants in South Africa (chapter 9) must have had combat experience and other skills that are useful to the South African forces.

"When I look at South African officers speaking Afrikaans or English, and during operations, I imagine that they will soon give orders in Hebrew," noted Israeli journalist Uri Dan in the Israeli journal *Monitin* of January 1982. Dan, a long-time confidant of former Defense Minister Ariel Sharon, was awed by the demeanor and energy of these valiant South Africans who reminded him so much of their Israeli counterparts. And in Pretoria, a senior officer told him, "Do not underestimate the example of the IDF as a fighting force to us." (p. 88).

The signature of Israeli counterinsurgency training has also been noticeable in recent years in the South African emphasis on practices such as gathering inside information within the guerilla organization and deep strikes into guerilla-held territory.[15] The South African invasion of Angola in early 1984, for instance, is said to have been modeled on the Israeli invasion of Lebanon in 1982. Under the February 1984 disengagement agreement, the Angolan government was to discourage South-West African People's Organization (SWAPO) guerilla activity against South Africa, while South Africa said it would do the same in regard to National Union for the Total Independence of Angola (UNITA). The proxy UNITA, headed by Jonas Savimbi, has continued to wage a war of sabotage and destruction aimed at overthrowing the Angolan government. Savimbi is believed to have received weapons and ammunition from Israel as well—by way of South Africa, as the October 12, 1985, *Daily Telegraph* reported from the scene.

The Israeli Mossad and the South African intelligence services are also cooperating closely and exchanging information on guerilla activities, among other matters. South Africa has reportedly gained access to Israeli sources in Africa and the United States, while Israel gained access to the Silvermine facility, an ultramodern surveillance center for naval vessels and aircraft.[16] So intimate are the ties that before Jonathan Pollard, the Israeli-recruited spy, was convicted of spying against the United States in 1987 Defense Secretary Caspar Weinberger reportedly prepared a sworn affidavit in which he detailed how Pollard had gravely compromised American intelligence operations—against South Africa. Pollard had fed Israel top-secret U.S. intelligence on South Africa, and Israel lost no time in passing it on to Pretoria, the CIA later found out. As a result, at least one, and possibly several, U.S. agents in South Africa were exposed, according to the same affidavit.[17]

An earlier incident, in 1983, involved the arrest of Commodore Dieter Gerhardt, commander of the Simonstown shipyard, where Israel and South Africa may have been cooperating on nuclear-powered submarines. The commodore was sentenced to life imprisonment and his wife to ten years in prison on charges of spying for the Soviet Union. It was also alleged at their trial that they had caused immense damage to—Israeli–South African relations.[18]

Another area of extensive cooperation between Israel and South Africa has been that of military electronics. The three largest Israeli electronics companies—Tadiran, Elbit, and Israel Aircraft Industries (IAI)—

have sold South Africa millions of dollars worth of equipment, most notably electronic fences, infiltration alarm systems, computers, communications systems, and night vision equipment for land and helicopters.[19] One electronic fence was erected in the late 1970s on the Angola-Namibia border in order to stop SWAPO guerillas. The fence, part of a project to surround South Africa with a "ring of steel," was built with IAI advanced technology.[20] When James Adams was writing his book, published in early 1984, the larger project was near completion; in areas where it was possible to travel, he noted, "the fifteen foot high fence is clearly visible with a cordon sanitaire running alongside."[21] The anti-personnel mines along the border area were also from Israel, he was told.

By now South Africa has its own electronics industry, which produces enough of certain items to export the surplus, among them field telephones, radios, and surveillance systems. Joint ventures with major Israeli companies have also been established, such as between South Africa's Consolidated Power and Tadiran, the Koor subsidiary. Their specialties are computers and military electronics. Another example is Conlog, formed by the Israeli company Elron and the Durban-based subsidiary of Control Logic.[22]

Among the most important products of the Israeli electronics industry is the Scout Remotely Piloted Vehicle (RPV), a pilotless aircraft crammed with advanced electronic equipment. During the summer of 1982, the RPV was very effective in detecting Syrian troop positions and jamming Syrian electronic equipment, thus helping destroy dozens of ground-to-air missiles. Having obtained the Israeli RPV, the South African forces can similarly detect guerilla bases in neighboring countries without risking any casualties. One such plane, reportedly with IAI markings, was shot down over Mozambique in mid-1983.[23]

Israel's arms exports, to which the Iran-Contra affair drew a great deal of attention, make up about one quarter of its total exports. That is among the highest ratios in the world. The sector is mostly government-owned, and the annual exports exceed $1 billion. More than one hundred industries and some 140,000 jobs or 10 percent of the labor force is involved: "The old image of a sunny Israel exporting oranges has been supplemented if not superseded by that of a small nation that can provide more bang for the buck."[24]

An interesting illustration of this dedication to provide "more bang for the buck" is a full page ad published by Israel Military Industries in the early 1980s (for example, *Aviation Week*, August 9, 1982). The ad shows an airplane loaded with bombs and assures the readers that the Israeli bombs are "bombs you can count on to do what they're supposed to do. That's the only kind of bomb we make." The Israeli bombs are made for "over 20 countries in the Free World," and additional juntas and governments are most welcome to "contact us before planning your next aircraft armament procurement program."

As to the above "Free World" customers, an Israeli journal notes that "the average purchaser of Israeli arms is most likely to be a non-industrialized country with a defense-oriented right wing government."[25] Not coincidentally, the Israeli directory of defense industries is published in Spanish as well as English.

When Israel seeks to export arms to South Africa and other countries with a "defense-oriented right wing government," its immediate objectives are to earn needed foreign exchange and recover part of the substantial investment in research and development that modern weapons require. Yet the destinations for these weapons are such that, as numerous authors have pointed out years before the Iran-contra scandal, a service is performed—by proxy—for United States power.[26] Thus Israel has regularly supplied weapons to countries such as Guatemala, Chile, Somoza's Nicaragua—and subsequently to the counterrevolutionaries[27]—at times when direct supplies from Washington would have been problematic. (Although the United States must be aware and at least implicitly approve of such transfers, it does not follow that every Israeli arms shipment is sent under instructions or after being cleared with Washington.)

Much the same seems to be true of Israeli–South African military ties, which have operated as an important conduit for arms and technology while Washington was in a position to say that it adhered to the UN embargo. Not surprisingly, at least in the Reagan years there have been no indications that the administration was troubled in any way by the Israeli ties with South Africa. The 1986 Comprehensive Anti-Apartheid Act indeed decreed that countries that sell arms to South Africa may lose U.S. Military assistance; but that was a Congressional initiative (which, in itself, crept unwanted into the legislation and which, in any event, no one believed would ever be applied to Israel). The U.S. *Executive* branch was more than willing to overlook the matter.

Israeli officials and lobbyists repeatedly remind Americans of Israel's varied usefulness to "American interests and security." In 1981 Yaakov Meridor, Menachem Begin's Special Assistant for Economic Coordination, was candid about the role his country was seeking to play: "We are going to say to the Americans," he explained in a speech before American and European businessmen, "Don't compete with us in Taiwan, South Africa, the Carribean, or in other countries where you couldn't directly do it [sell arms]. You sell ammunition and equipment by proxy. Israel will be your proxy." [28]

That same year, after his visit to the "operational areas" in Namibia, Defense Minister Ariel Sharon came to Washington to sign the Memorandum of Understanding on Strategic Cooperation with the Reagan administration. Sharon openly urged that the UN embargo be broken because of what he described as South Africa's urgent need for weapons to stop Communism. [29]

Although South African officials often talk about "self-sufficiency," ARMSCOR has a long way to go before it can produce on its own all the heavy weapons and electronics the South African military needs. South Africa is hardly "self-sufficient" in modern aircraft production and large ships, for instance. It needs spare parts for weapons already supplied and can certainly use advice on how best to counter modern Soviet equipment. Again, Israel has had much to offer. According to the Stockholm International Peace Research Institute, South Africa was Israel's leading arms customer in the 1970s, the destination for more than 35 percent of Israel's exports. [30] In 1982 Israeli officials said that the junta in Argentina was the second largest recipient of Israeli arms supplies, with South Africa at the top. [31] The same figures are available from a recent study by Dr. Aaron Klieman of Tel Aviv University's Jaffe Center for Strategic Studies. [32] The South African purchases included naval vessels, anti-tank missiles, air-to-air missiles and radar equipment. More recently, South Africa is reported to have purchased from Israel helicopters, tear gas and smoke gas.

By the mid-1980s Israeli–South African military ties assumed the character of a partnership; the focus of this "cosiest of all [of Israel's military relationships]," as the July 20, 1985, *Economist* described it, shifted from direct South African purchases of finished equipment to technology transfers, joint research, co-production and licensing, often after initial financing by South Africa. Weapons produced by ARMSCOR, from assault rifles to missiles and ships are virtually identical to the Israeli originals. (The names are different.) This has not kept Israeli spokesmen from dismissing reports of close Israeli–South African military ties on grounds that most of South Africa's defense needs are met by domestic production.

In 1986, according to unofficial estimates cited in the *New York Times*, Israel earned anywhere from $400 million to $800 million from the export of military equipment and technology to South Africa (chapter 5).

The most widely reported South African military purchase from Israel is the Reshef patrol ship. Under the 1955 Simonstown agreement, Britain supplied South Africa with patrol ships in order to control the Cape Sea route. But when the agreement was canceled in 1975 South Africa found itself with little ship-building experience and turned to Israel to fill the gap. During his trip to Israel in 1976, Vorster agreed to purchase three Israeli Reshef missile-firing ships and manufacture nine more under license in Durban. (This according to *The Unnatural Alliance*; other sources report that six were built in Israel.) The Reshefs (renamed "Minister") are equipped with sea-to-sea Gabriel missiles (renamed "Scorpion"), also manufactured in South Africa under Israeli license. The guns for the ships were made in Italy; because of the arms embargo, Israel acted as middleman.[33] To complete the deal, South African naval personnel were trained in Israel in the use of the new equipment, a fact reported in the Israeli press as well.[34] While in Israel, the children of the South Africans are said to have attended an Afrikaans school established specially for them.

South Africa also purchased six Israeli, Dvora-type, fast patrol ships and may have agreed to help finance the next generation of Israeli warships, an ultramodern version of the Reshef.[35] In addition, according to the 1983–1984 edition of the *International Security Yearbook*, ARMSCOR was to produce several 1,200-ton corvettes modeled on the Israeli, Aliyah-class vessels.

Another agreement reached during Vorster's 1976 visit pertained to armor development. (As noted, military cooperation increased sharply after that visit; South African military spending was raised by 40 percent shortly before Vorster left for Israel.[36]) South Africa had the specially hardened steel the Israelis had long sought in order to sheath their Merkava tanks; with Israeli know-how the South African steel was turned into formidable armor not only for the Merkava tanks but also for most armored vehicles used by the South African army, which were rendered highly resistant to anti-tank weapons. In addition, Israel agreed to modernize 150 South African Centurion tanks.[37]

South Africa is now in possession of one of the most sophisticated artillery systems in the world, a 155mm howitzer that can double as a nuclear delivery system. The item, manufactured by Space Research Corporation of Vermont, was smuggled to South Africa in the mid-1970s in one of the most serious violations of the arms embargo. It was a complex laundering operation that involved re-exporting the hardware and the technology from Israel with the assistance of state-owned Israel Military Industries (IMI) as well as other organizations and governments. Two SRC executives were eventually fined and given short prison terms. The howitzer filled a large gap in South Africa's military needs and is now even available as one of South Africa's "own" exports.[38]

Israel has also done a great deal for the South African air force. South Africa can build French Mirage fighters under license, but these are increasingly outmoded. The state-of-the-art aircraft it seeks are no longer available from Western governments, and unlike lighter weapons cannot easily be smuggled or purchased through middlemen. "The answer," said a report in the September 14, 1984, *Times* of London, "is likely to be increasingly close cooperation with Israel."

The increasingly close cooperation had in fact been going on for years. Israeli air force officers regularly lectured before their South African counterparts on combat against Soviet aircraft and Soviet-trained pilots; they helped the South African air force build modern, efficient air bases; other Israeli experts updated the equipment of the South African Mirages. When the South Africans needed Mirage spare parts, which France often refused to supply due to the arms embargo, Israeli technicians stationed in South Africa performed the repairs and maintenance using spare parts from Israeli warehouses. Some of the repairs were so complex that under normal circumstances the manufacturer would have been called in.[39]

The Israeli Kfir jet, an improved and modernized version of the Mirage (in fact built with stolen Mirage III plans) would be an ideal purchase for South Africa: It is not expected to become obsolete until the mid 1990s, and because of its similarity to the original Mirage requires no significant retooling or retraining of pilots. But the Kfirs used by the Israeli air force are powered by General Electric engines and could not be sold to South Africa without U.S. permission—unless the engines and other parts were replaced.

In the summer of 1985, the *Economist* reported that Israel had sold South Africa at least thirty-six Kfirs.[40] A year later the South African air force unveiled the Cheetah, an updated version of the Mirage. Predictably, it turned out that the Israeli allies had lent a generous hand: The Cheetah "bears uncanny resemblance to the IAI Kfir" and was indeed built "in collaboration with IAI," *Jane's Defence Weekly* reported on July 27, 1986. IAI built the weapons system of the Cheetah, while a subsidiary of IAI was responsible for its navigation system.

In November 1986, following the imposition of additional European and American sanctions against Pretoria, the London *Sunday Telegraph* reported about a striking Israeli "sanctions busting" delivery to South Africa: two aircraft refueling tankers of the type that had made it possible for the United States to bomb Libya the previous April. Analysts described the sale as a "dramatic breakthrough" that will allow the South African air force to strike virtually anywhere in sub-Saharan Africa, including Zambia and Tanzania on the eastern coast of the continent, "the heart of the ANC's (African National Congress) operations." The improved strike power of the SAAF has increased regional tensions and led Zimbabwe to request sophisticated Soviet equipment.[41]

NOTES

1. James Adams, *The Unnatural Alliance* (London: Quartet Books, 1984), p. 26.

2. Thomas Friedman, "Israelis Reassess Supplying Arms to South Africa," *New York Times*, January 29, 1987, p. A1, and "Israel Parliament Hears Plan on Pretoria," March 20, 1987, p. A3; Yossi Melman and Dan Raviv, "Has Congress Doomed Israel's Affair With South Africa?" *Washington Post*, February 22, 1987, p. C1; Wolf Blitzer, "U.S. Report Concludes: Israel, France, Italy Sold Pretoria Arms 'Regularly'," *Jerusalem Post*, April 2, 1987, p. 1. Still more details about the nearly symbiotic military cooperation can be found in Benjamin Beit-Hallahmi's *The Israeli Connection: Who Israel Arms and Why* (New York: Pantheon, 1987), p. 108–74.

3. Adams, *The Unnatural Alliance,* p. 125.

4. Richard Leonard, *South Africa at War: White Power and the Crisis in Southern Africa* (Westport, Conn.: Lawrence Hill & Co., 1983), pp. 131–37; United States House of Representatives, International Relations Committee,

Subcommittee on Africa, "United States-South African Relations: Arms Embargo Implementation," Testimony by Sean Gervasi, H 461-74.1, July 14, 1977, pp. 2–41.

5. Andrew Pierre, *The Global Politics of Arms Sales* (Princeton: Princeton University Press, 1982), pp. 266–67.

6. Olusola Ojo, "Israeli–South Africa Connections and Afro-Israeli Relations," *International Studies*, January-March, 1982, p. 46.

7. *Davar*, December 17, 1982; *New York Times*, December 5, 1982, p. 7.

8. Jack Penn, "South Africa/Israel Cooperation in War," *Armed Forces* (South Africa, February 1981).

9. Letter from former Knesset Member Yedidia Beeri in rebuttal to Naomi Chazan's contention that Israel has benefited little from the ties with South Africa. *Haaretz*, August 16, 1985.

10. Penn, "South Africa/Israel Cooperation," p. 12.

11. Adams, *The Unnatural Alliance*, p. 33.

12. "Israel Held Giving S. Africa Military Information," *Washington Post*, July 8, 1975; Zdenek Cervenka and Barbara Rogers, *The Nuclear Axis: Secret Collaboration Between West Germany and South Africa* (New York: Times Books, 1978), p. 410.

13. Rosalyne Ainslee, "Israel and South Africa: An Unlikely Alliance?," United Nations Department of Political and Security Affairs, 1981, p. 12.

14. Adams, *The Unnatural Alliance*, p. 80. On Marcia Friedman's question in the Knesset, see also *New York Times*, June 1, 1976, p. 9.

15. Adams, *The Unnatural Alliance*, p. 90. See also Philip Frankel, *Pretoria's Praetorians: Civil-Military Relations in South Africa* (New York: Cambridge University Press, 1984). Frankel points out that "many South African officers take their cues from the Israelis in the process of putting total strategy into operations" (p. 66).

16. Adams, *The Unnatural Alliance*, p. 86.

17. *Sunday Times* (London) and the *Jerusalem Post*, March 29, 1987.

18. *Washington Post*, February 22, 1987, p. C2.

19. *The Economist*, November 5, 1977, p. 90.

20. Israel Shahak, *Israel's Global Role: Weapons for Repression*. (Belmont, Mass.: Association of Arab-American University Graduates, 1981), p. 28, citing a 1980 lecture by Colin Legum. On November 2, 1977 *Foreign Report* (published by the London *Economist*) noted that work was already in progress on an Israeli-style "electronic wall."

21. Adams, *The Unnatural Alliance*, p. 93.

22. Z. Shapiro, "A Study of Some of the Factors Influencing the Use of Israel as a Springboard for South African Exports," Graduate School of Business, University of Cape Town, MBA Thesis, 1979, p. 18.

23. *New Africa*, August 1983; *The Christian Science Monitor*, June 6, 1983;

Washington Post, February 22, 1987, p. C2. See also a report in *Jane's Defence Weekly*, September 27, 1986.

24. "Israel Said to Depend Heavily on Arms Sales," *Washington Post*, March 22, 1985, p. E1. Also Hanan Nobil, "Selling Defense," *Israel Economist*, July 1984, p. 21.

25. Nobil, "Selling Defense."

26. Esther Howard, "Israel: The Sorcerer's Apprentice," *MERIP Reports*, February 1983; Shahak, *Israel's Global Role*, passim; Azim Husain, "The West, South Africa and Israel: A Strategic Triangle," *Third World Quarterly* 4, no. 1, January 1982. For full details on Israel's relationships with repressive Third World regimes and an analysis of a range of hypotheses to explain them see Benjamin Beit-Hallahmi's *The Israeli Connection*.

27. For reports that preceded the Iran-Contra arms scandal, see for instance the *New York Times* on January 5 and January 13, 1985. More recent information provided by David K. Shipler, "Israel and the Contras: Denials Are Questioned," *New York Times*, December 5, 1986, p. 13.

28. *Financial Times*, August 18, 1981; *Haaretz*, August 25, 1981, p. 11.

29. *New York Times*, December 14, 1981.

30. Stockholm International Peace Research Institute, *World Armament and Disarmament: SIPRI Yearbook* (London: Taylor & Francis, Ltd., 1981), p. 116. A good summary of reported Israeli–South African military as well as other dealings in the 1970s can be found in a February 10, 1978 *New York Times* story, "Israeli Tours South Africa as Arms Trade Furor Grows."

31. *New York Times*, May 9, 1982, p. 16.

32. Aaron S. Klieman, *Israel's Global Reach: Arms Sales as Diplomacy* (Washington: Pergamon-Brassey's, 1985), also reported in the *Washington Post*, "Israel Said to Depend Heavily on Arms Sales," March 22, 1985, p. E1.

33. "Strangers and Brothers: The Unlikely Alliance Between Israel and South Africa," by editors of the *Sunday Times* (London), April 15, 1984.

34. *Maariv*, August 6, 1976; *New York Times*, August 18, 1976.

35. *Economist*, November 5, 1977, p. 90.

36. Major Gerald Keller (USMC), "Israeli–South African Trade: An Analysis of Recent Developments," *Naval War College Review*, Spring 1978, p. 70.

37. *Economist*, November 5, 1977, p. 90.

38. Adams, *The Unnatural Alliance*, pp. 38–71. See also *The Middle East* (London), April 1981, pp. 27–30.

39. *The Times* (London), October 29, 1981.

40. "Israel Survey," *Economist*, July 20, 1985, p. 17.

41. *Sunday Telegraph* (London), November 16, 1986, p. 1, and *New York Newsday*, November 25, 1986, p. 13. The *Sunday Telegraph* reported on November 15, 1987, that Israeli electronic countermeasures were protecting South African planes in an offensive against Angola.

CHAPTER 7

The Ultimate Weapon: "Don't Push Us Too Far!"

Something will happen that the proponents of violence cannot even dream of . . . They don't know what they are going to reap . . . A big silence and desolation will come over many parts of South Africa.

—P. W. Botha, in Parliament, 1982.[1]

South Africa provided coal, steel, and uranium in return for Israeli military products.

—From a 1985 study coauthored by Amnon Neubach, economic Advisor to Prime Minister Peres.[2]

While the Israeli–South African commercial and military ties have been frequently criticized and condemned at the United Nations, by far the greatest source of concern in recent years has been the evident nuclear collaboration between these two besieged countries, each situated in a major world hot spot. The specter of a beleaguered, white minority government armed with weapons of mass destruction and sophisticated delivery systems is a threat even to those Africans situated thousands of miles from South Africa.

Nor is it reassuring to recall that South Africa, like Israel, has been unwilling to sign the Non-Proliferation Treaty, which would have subjected its nuclear facilities to International Atomic Energy Agency inspections. To be sure, such inspections are far from foolproof; that makes it all the more significant when a government refuses to accept a measure of international monitoring. One hundred and twenty three countries have joined the superpowers and Britain as signatories of the

1968 treaty. The list stretches alphabetically from Afghanistan to Zaire, including Libya; the other non-signatories outside the official nuclear club are India, Pakistan, Argentina, and Brazil.[3]

Cooperation to develop nuclear weapons, which is the highest form of cooperation between any two states and requires the greatest amount of trust, is, understandably, also the most closely guarded secret of this relationship. The amount of circumstantial evidence may be impressive, but those who insist on documented ''proof'' are not likely to be satisfied. A 1980 United Nations report—gleefully quoted by some supporters of Israel—acknowledges that since ''there have been no official statements to confirm such cooperation in the nuclear field . . . this whole question remains in a state of uncertainty'' until ''specific examples of actual nuclear exchanges or transactions can be cited as clear evidence of such cooperation.''[4] (Nonetheless—and this is not to be found in literature distributed by supporters of Israel—given the circumstantial evidence, the General Assembly of the UN has repeatedly called in its resolutions for an end to the ''continuing and increasing collaboration of Israel with the racist regime of South Africa, especially in the military and nuclear fields.'')

What is beyond dispute is that South Africa has vast quantities of uranium, quantities exceeded only by the United States and Canada. South Africa controls large empty areas suitable for nuclear tests and, in addition, has access to the Indian Ocean. Israel, according to the familiar pattern, has none of the above but does have the know-how to complement these assets.

For other pariah states, a military defeat might mean ''only'' a change of regime. In the case of South Africa and Israel, planners cannot be so sure. Can the United States absolutely be *counted on* to intervene on their behalf if worst comes to worst?[5] For them, the question almost answers itself when the fate of South Vietnam is recalled. But few small nations can produce all the modern weapons they need, and even if they could, the supplies might not last through a protracted war. In the case of Israel, there is also widespread concern about the narrowing ''technology gap'' and the rising military strength of some Arab states, most notably Syria. ''Unless one assumes a racial theory of Arab inferiority,'' noted Steven J. Rosen in *Nuclear Proliferation and the Near-Nuclear Countries*, ''tiny Israel's past victories against the populous Arab world must be regarded as somewhat 'unnatural' events to be explained by special circumstances.''[6]

That some Israelis already favor "going public" with the bomb as the ultimate guarantee that their country will not end up like the Crusaders is hardly surprising. Shai Feldman of Tel Aviv University is among the better-known proponents of this option.[7] In a 1976 address, Moshe Dayan also pointed to the "absurdity of turning Israel into a warehouse of (conventional) hardware" and proposed instead to put Israel's nuclear cards on the table.[8]

But most Israeli public statements on this matter have been ambiguous, neither confirming nor flatly denying the possession of nuclear weapons. In 1974 President Ephraim Katzir, a distinguished scientist himself, said that Israel would not be the first country to deploy nuclear weapons in the Middle East but has the potential to do so if necessary[9]; in a 1981 interview with the *New York Times*, Dayan repeated that Israel can deploy such weapons in a short time if necessary, leaving a clear impression that it would not be starting from scratch.[10]

By now, the phrase "Israel will not be the first . . . etc." has become a ritual response nearly every time Israeli officials are asked about nuclear weapons. The tired formula was repeated in the fall of 1986 even after Mordechai Vanunu, a former employee of the Dimona nuclear facility, provided details and photographs of Israeli nuclear weapons to the October 5 *Sunday Times* of London. He also told reporters in the British capital about frequent exchanges of visits between Israeli and South African nuclear scientists. Later on, Vanunu found himself in Israel, after apparently being kidnapped by Mossad agents. His trial is pending at this writing.

Like Israelis, South African whites are aware that they cannot afford a defeat. "I am afraid we can lose only once," Chief of the Army Lieutenant General Magnus Malan once said.[11] Under the assumption of rational planning, however, it is not immediately clear why Pretoria would want nuclear weapons. The main threat to the white government comes from within; no nuclear weapon can prevent or stop mass insurgency, although a neutron device that destroys only living things might have a demoralizing effect. Further, a nuclear South Africa would likely be subject to more severe Western sanctions and possibly have Soviet missiles pointed at it. But there are also substantial benefits to going nuclear, among them an improved bargaining position vis-à-vis intimidated black states, which understand once and for all that confrontation is futile. Alternately, under the nuclear umbrella, Pretoria could feel even freer to continue to invade and subvert its neighbors. But above all, the payoffs would be psychological, no small matter for a besieged white minority uncertain of its future. "Don't push us too far!" President P. W. Botha warned the outside world in an August 15, 1985 address on South Africa's future.

Turning to nuclear potentials, Israel has had the sophisticated Dimona reactor in the Negev desert since the late 1950s. At first Ben-Gurion claimed it was a "textile factory," but in 1960 a U-2 spy plane confirmed American suspicions about the nature of the facility. Since Israel has not signed the Non-Proliferation Treaty, no outside inspectors may enter the heavily-guarded facility. It is likely that plutonium was produced there and used to build nuclear weapons; by the early 1970s the Central Intelligence Agency, as well as other Western intelligence services, indeed concluded that Israel possessed the ultimate weapon.[12] Thus one now-declassified CIA memorandum dated September 4, 1974, stated: "We believe that Israel already has produced nuclear weapons," citing Israeli efforts to obtain large quantities of uranium, often by "clandestine means," ambiguous Israeli efforts in the field of uranium enrichment, and Israel's substantial investment in the "Jericho" missile system, which can accomodate nuclear warheads.

The above "clandestine means," according to *The Unnatural Alliance* and numerous other reports,[13] included hijackings of uranium shipments in Europe by Mossad agents, smuggling operations, and the establishing of dummy companies that purchased uranium and then diverted it to Israel. One of the better-known cases was the disappearance of some 200 pounds of uranium from the Nuclear Materials and Equipment Corporation (NUMEC) in Pennsylvania in the mid-1960s. The company, headed by Zalman Shapiro, a devout supporter of Israel, was also under contract to be that country's "technical consultant and training procurement center" in the United States. In 1967 Zalman Shapiro was fined $1.1 million in connection with the disappearance of the uranium. Where the uranium must have ended up, and for what purpose, was no mystery to most experts.[14] Deputy Director of the CIA for Science and Technology Carl Duckett was later quoted on ABC Television as confirming that his agency had reached the same conclusion: The stolen uranium was being used to build atomic weapons in Israel.[15]

Another widely reported Mossad operation was the spectacular diversion to Israel of the contents of an entire ship loaded with 200 tons of uranium. In 1968 the *Scheersberg* left Rotterdam for Genoa, without ever reaching its destination. When it reappeared, it had a new name and crew—but no cargo. The barrels with the uranium had been transferred in mid-sea to a heavily escorted Israeli ship.[16]

But that was no way to get uranium in the long run. A more dependable source had to be found, and was—South Africa. "Now that Israel can no longer rely on hijacking uranium shipments, there can be little doubt that the Israelis regard South Africa as a vitally important source of uranium, both natural and enriched, free of any international safeguards or inspection."[17]

South Africa's nuclear potential rests on a foundation set by several Western countries in the 1950s and 1960s. In those years the United States, Britain, West Germany, and France readily supplied materials, technology, and training for South African scientists. Nuclear cooperation with the United States began in the early 1950s with the development of the mining and processing industry in South Africa.[18] In 1957 the Eisenhower administration signed the fifty-year "Atoms for Peace" cooperation agreement with Pretoria. Under the agreement South Africa received the Safari-1 nuclear reactor in 1961, followed by approximately 200 pounds of enriched uranium. By 1967 another reactor, Safari-2 (now decommissioned) was developed in South Africa, this time with Israeli assistance as well.[19] South Africa also obtained a nuclear reactor from France (at Koeberg) and a pilot uranium enrichment plant from West Germany (at Valindaba). Israeli scientists and technicians have regularly visited these facilities.[20]

One of the most distinguished Israeli visitors was Ernst David Bergman, who probably has the best claim to the title of "father" of Israel's nuclear capability. Bergman, a close associate of Chaim Weizmann and David Ben-Gurion, headed the science department of the Israeli Defense Ministry for twenty years. In addition, between 1953 and 1966 he was chairman of the Israeli Atomic Energy Commission.[21] In 1968, the year he visited South Africa, Bergman was awarded the Israel Prize for Natural Sciences. In a keynote speech before the South African Institute of International Affairs, he discussed the "common problems" that Israel and South Africa experienced and the need for both to remain technologically superior. Cooperation was both possible and desirable, Bergman concluded. The address deserves some attention because it was delivered around the time that Israeli–South

African scientific and nuclear cooperation began to expand, and because the speaker was a prominent Israeli who enthusiastically pledged to do his very best to further such cooperation.

The lengthy address did not make a single reference to the political situation in the country with which Bergman was eager to accelerate cooperation, but it did include insights such as the following, with respect to educational gaps between populations within each country: "of course our problem is a little easier than that of your country because the Jews coming from Arab countries, although they have been reduced to the intellectual level of the Arab countries, have a tradition for learning and respect for learning."

Turning to what South Africa and Israel can do for each other, he explained:

It is difficult to indicate . . . whether South Africa or Israel is the more highly developed. I think that in both countries the development is uneven—there are many areas in which Israel undoubtedly can learn from South Africa . . . There are areas in which Israel has been forced to be more progressive and in which perhaps a country like South Africa could learn from her . . . I have discussed with many of my colleagues whom I have met in this country and with whom I have created some personal and professional links the question whether, in view of the circumstances, a collaboration between the two countries might not be of some value. I was glad to find a very enthusiastic response and the willingness to think about the exchange of professors, the exchange of graduate students, and the exchange of information, and in going back to Israel I will do my best to further and perhaps formalize such contacts between scientists of our two countries.[22]

The opportunity must not be missed: "Neither of us has neighbors to whom we can speak and to whom we are going to be able to speak in the near future. If we are in this position of isolation, perhaps it might be best for both our countries to speak to each other."

Like the Israeli leadership, the South Africans have dropped numerous nuclear hints, without saying anything explicit. By 1974 Dr. L. Alberts, vice president of South Africa's Atomic Energy Board, was in a position to say that "our technology and science have advanced sufficiently for us to produce an atomic bomb if we have to,"[23] and a month after returning from Israel, Prime Minister Vorster repeated, also ambiguously, that "we can enrich uranium and we have the capability. And we did not sign the Nuclear Non-Proliferation Treaty."[24]

In August 1977, a Soviet satellite detected signs of South African preparations for a nuclear test in the Kalahari desert. The information was shared with the United States government, which found it to be correct, as did the British, West German, and French intelligence services. All four Western countries then warned Pretoria of serious consequences, including severing diplomatic relations, should such a test take place. The test was averted.[25] The following month, in the September 12 issue, *Newsweek* quoted a high-ranking official in Washington who said: "I know some intelligence people who are convinced with damn near certainty it was an Israeli nuclear device." Others did not go quite that far, thinking that the device was South African and Israel had merely helped build it. A query to Prime Minister Vorster's office about these suspicions produced only a terse "no comment." The aborted explosion may have been a contributing factor to the arms embargo resolution passed by the United Nations later that year.

Systematic exchanges of materials and nuclear technology between South Africa and Israel apparently began after Vorster's visit in 1976. A 1979 study by the United States Defense Intelligence Agency found that Israeli scientists were working on nuclear projects in South Africa, as South Africa was supplying uranium to Israel and Taiwan. This was an outcome of the "enhanced international opportunities in the nuclear field from the emerging pariah state network"—in addition to the full web of other military and economic ties between these states.[26]

These "enhanced opportunities" seem to have led to an event which has since become the most talked-about feature of South African–Israeli nuclear cooperation. On the night of September 22, 1979, a United States Vela satellite, which was circling the earth expressly in order to monitor compliance with the 1963 nuclear Test Ban Treaty, registered a double light flash as it was passing over the Indian Ocean near the Prince Edward islands. A double light flash is almost invariably the mark of a nuclear explosion. The satellite had an error-free record, its sophisticated instruments having registered 41 out of 41 previous nuclear tests. Also, the area where the double flash was detected is ideal for secret nuclear explosions since it is deserted and characterized by a high degree of natural radiation. It so happened that South Africa was in the process of conducting a secret naval exercise in that same area, and the Central Intelligence Agency knew it.[27]

The Vela discovery was kept secret for several weeks until it was reported on American television newscasts. The reports were followed by widespread speculation that South Africa and Israel had joined the nuclear club. Both governments dismissed the reports, although three days after the flash, Prime Minister Botha warned ''terrorists'' that ''we have military weapons they do not know about.'' [28]

In early 1980 Dan Raviv, the CBS correspondent in Israel, learned about a manuscript just completed by two Israeli journalists, Ami Dor-On, and Eli Teicher. It was titled *None Will Survive Us: The Story of the Israeli A-Bomb*, and, among other matters, confirmed the speculations about the nature of the explosion. In February Raviv flew to Rome to avoid Israeli censorship and reported about the new book. As a result, the Israeli authorities revoked Raviv's press credentials, an unexpected reaction to the reporting of ''nonsense,'' as the above reports had been described by officials. The book itself, apparently written as a novel, was banned by the Israeli censor; the authors were warned that if they defy the ban they could be imprisoned for a period from fifteen years to life. [29]

In the United States, President Jimmy Carter decided to appoint a distinguished commission of inquiry to determine what had really happened. The commission, headed by Dr. Jack Ruina of the Massachusetts Institute of Technology completed its investigation in November 1979, but the report was not released until the following July, and even then it was a sanitized version. For the commission, the key factor was the absence of a ''smoking gun'' in the form of nuclear radiation and unique shock waves. It therefore turned to consider naturally-occurring atmospheric events that might have caused the Vela instruments to register a double flash: ''Although we cannot rule out the possibility that this signal was of nuclear origin, the panel considers it more likely that the signal was one of the zoo events, possibly a consequence of the impact of a small meteoroid on the satellite.'' [30] The term ''zoo event'' referred to a random occurence, the truth about which may never be known. The White House scientists did not determine that there had been no nuclear explosion, as it is sometimes falsely alleged.

The final report not only satisfied the calls for an official inquiry; it averted a foreign policy disaster for President Carter in an election year when the Iran hostage crisis was very nearly all the political headache he could handle. The Carter administration, which regarded non-proliferation as a major foreign policy goal, was spared having to answer questions about the role of the United States in Israeli and South African nuclear capabilities, or about U.S. monitoring competence, the latter a crucial factor in arms control. Had Israel been found to have carried out a nuclear explosion, the president would have had to cut off aid and any nuclear transactions with it under non-proliferation legislation and the Symington Amendment; the Camp David deal of which Carter was so proud would have been in danger while a nuclear arms race in the Middle East would have become a realistic prospect.

Politicians in Washington and elsewhere then had reason to be satisfied with what was believed to be the last word about the explosion. But a good number of scientists, intelligence officials and investigative journalists were less certain. In fact, they regarded the findings of the panel as hasty and evasive. To start with, as a UN study asked, given the record and accuracy of the satellite, should the panel not have considered the possibility that the absence of ''hot trails'' was suggestive of successful efforts to disguise the explosion rather than no explosion?[31] Typical of the panelists' hasty dismissal of indications pointing to a nuclear explosion was, according to some critics, the handling of information about a ripple in the atmosphere detected on the night in question by the world's largest radio telescope at Arecibo, Puerto Rico. There were no earthquakes or other natural causes to readily explain the ripple, whose timing and direction corresponded to the Vela findings. The White House panel questioned the competence of Arecibo scientists to conduct accurate measurements of such phenomena; besides, the instruments might after all have recorded a tropical storm near Arecibo, the commission said. ''It surprised me,'' one Arecibo scientist commented later, ''that people have tried as much as they did to discredit it.''[32] A double flash and an ionospheric ripple occurring simultaneously are indeed an astonishing coincidence.

More importantly, the Defense Intelligence Agency, the CIA, the Department of the Navy, Los Alamos Laboratory scientists (where Vela was developed), and the Naval Research Laboratory conducted parallel investigations. All of these investigations concluded that a nuclear explosion had occurred.[33] The CIA named Israel and South Africa as partners in the explosion. Another of the discordant voices which, according to *Science* magazine, ''continue to rise above the White House mood music whose theme is that nothing happened and if something did it cannot be proved"[34] was a report by a staff of seventy-five researchers at the Naval Research Laboratory.

Similarly, an extensive report published in the London monthly *The Middle East* in June 1980 found, after interviewing more than two dozen officials, "an astonishing accumulation of circumstantial evidence suggesting that there was indeed a nuclear blast." Not all past nuclear tests left measurable fallout; the United States began to search for radioactivity at least three days after the double flash, time enough for radiation from a low-yield explosion to have dissipated even if its exact area in the middle of the ocean could be pinpointed; further, there had been no "zoo events" in the previous decade.[35] Others asked why the commission had failed to consider the possibility of a neutron bomb, which leaves no fallout but produces the same double flash.[36]

Foreign Report, published by the London *Economist*, learned that President Carter had not advised the commission about intelligence reports on nuclear cooperation between Israel, South Africa, and Taiwan. Some of these reports, based on intercepted messages and documents, confirmed that Israeli nuclear scientists were working in South Africa. It was also learned that in March 1980 Israeli Defense Minister Ezer Weizmann flew to South Africa on state business.[37] The Israeli censor first granted permission—which it shortly afterwards withdrew—to broadcast a report that Weizman had spent three days discussing "security matters" in South Africa.[38]

Another possibly relevant fact was disclosed by the National Technical Information Service to the U.S. Senate Special Subcommittee on Nuclear Proliferation: the South African Defense and Naval Attaché in Washington had shown keen interest in literature on "detection of nuclear explosions and countermeasures to prevent detection," including the flight path of Vela. He requested a computer search of such sources, the only request of this kind ever received.[39]

Still more information became available in the spring of 1985. After a five-year investigation, columnist Jack Anderson confirmed that United States intelligence agencies have known since 1979 that a South African–Israeli nuclear test took place. This fact too was not shared with the White House panel, although it was disclosed in secret testimony to the National Security Council and to Congress, Anderson says.[40]

In May 1985 the Washington Office on Africa, in cooperation with Congressman John Conyers' office and the Congressional Black Caucus Foundation completed a study which reached similar conclusions about the nature of the explosion. This time some 500 pages of previously unreleased documents were obtained through the Freedom of Information Act. The documents led the U.S. Naval Research Laboratory to the "firm conclusion that a nuclear explosion had indeed occurred" after the "most extensive study by any agency in the U.S. government on this matter."[41] Among the new pieces of evidence was a letter written by a University of Tennessee professor to the Naval Research Laboratory. Shortly after the time of the blast, the professor was in Australia conducting research on sheep thyroids. He was surprised to find unusually high levels of radioactive iodine in them, a first in his twenty-five years of research. The Naval Research Laboratory and the National Oceanic and Atmospheric Administration confirmed that wind and weather patterns at the site of the explosion were such that fallout might have reached Australia. The White House panel was unaware of these findings, to which no alternative explanation has been proposed.

All the above evidence remains circumstantial, but its scope is impressive—and growing. And if the event was a nuclear blast, might South Africa have acted alone? A State Department official told the *Washington Post* in 1980: "It basically comes down to a choice between South Africa and Israel—or both."[42] But, as James Adams observed: "It is, of course, rather difficult to distinguish between an Israeli and a South African bomb. It is certainly true that South Africa has developed her own deterrent on her own soil, but the work has been done with the help of Israeli scientists and Israeli technology."[43]

How a nuclear device might be delivered is another significant question. Both countries can use their high-performance aircraft and Jericho missiles. But according to some reports, their nuclear cooperation extends to the development of cruise missiles, with Taiwan as a third partner. Jack Anderson noted in 1980 that "United States intelligence agencies had known for years that the three nations were working together on nuclear weapons development. But the addition of cruise missiles to their arsenals drastically alters the worldwide 'balance of terror'."[44]

Two Minutes Over Bagdad, a book about the 1981 Israeli bombing of the unfinished Iraqi nuclear reactor, lends additional weight to the numerous reports about Israeli–South African nuclear cooperation.[45] The book is significant because of the background of its three authors:

Amos Perlmutter, a former member of the Israeli Atomic Energy Commission and of the Israeli delegation to the United Nations who is now professor of political science and sociology at American University in Washington; Uri Bar-Yosef, a former Israeli air force officer; Michael Handel, a military historian at the Harvard Center for International Affairs. (At the time of the bombing, the Begin government claimed the right for a preemptive strike on grounds that the facility could be used to produce nuclear weapons in defiance of the Non-Proliferation Treaty to which Iraq, unlike Israel, was a signatory.) *Two Minutes Over Bagdad* deals primarily with the destruction of the reactor, but also recalls that during the 1973 war Israel made preparations and warned Washington that it would use nuclear weapons unless it received the American weapons it wanted. Since the early 1970s, the authors say, Israel has been working to expand its tactical and strategic nuclear arsenal in cooperation with South Africa and Taiwan. They note without comment that the CIA and other Western intelligence services concluded that the September 1979 explosion was caused by a nuclear shell launched by South Africa and Israel. Perlmutter, Bar-Yosef, and Handel then cite Jack Anderson's report about a cruise missile with a range of 1,500 miles that South Africa, Israel, and Taiwan were developing. Such a missile could strike almost anywhere in the Arab world and even reach parts of the Soviet Union.[46]

Reports pointing to Israeli–South African nuclear cooperation continued to appear through the end of 1986. According to a front-page story in the December 28 London *Observer*, South Africa was planning to build a 4 million Sterling Pound runway as part of developing Marion Island, a remote Antarctic territory. Strategic experts, such as Dr. Frank Barnaby, former director of the Stockholm International Peace Research Institute, believe that the area could be used for testing nuclear missiles. Predictably, scientists on the island have reported visits by Israeli and South African military officers. Two of the Israelis were in the team that surveyed the proposed runway site.

Israel has also agreed to participate in the "Star Wars" project after being invited to do so along with a handful of close United States allies. The *Jerusalem Post* defense correspondent Hirsh Goodman was enthusiastic: The scheme was "something to be grateful for" since it offers, among other benefits, "potentially real answers to this country's economic and defense needs." The system could, for instance, "render it unnecessary to bomb the next Iraqi reactor."[47]

NOTES

1. P. W. Botha in Parliament in February 1982, as quoted by James North in *Freedom Rising: War and Peace in Southern Africa* (New York: Macmillan, 1985), p. 323. The author believes that Botha was referring to a neutron bomb that destroys only living things, not property, and that a totalitarian government cannot be counted on to act rationally when cornered.

2. Yoram Peri and Amnon Neubach, *The Military-Industrial Complex in Israel: A Pilot Study* (Tel Aviv: International Center for Peace in the Middle East, 1985), p. 76. There are no nuclear power plants in Israel.

3. Mohamed Shaker, *The Non-Proliferation Treaty* (Dobbs Ferry, N.Y.: Oceana Publishers, 1980), appendix; Leonard Spector, "Proliferation: The Silent Spread," *Foreign Policy*, no. 58, Spring 1985. France and China have not signed the treaty, citing objections to its "discriminatory" treatment of non-nuclear weapons states.

4. United Nations General Assembly, Report of the Secretary General, "Implementation of the Declaration on the Denuclearization of Africa," Document #A/35/402, September 1980, p. 17.

5. Robert Harkavy, "Pariah States and Nuclear Proliferation," in George H. Quester, ed., *Nuclear Proliferation: Breaking the Chain* (Madison, Wis.: University of Wisconsin Press, 1981), p. 143.

6. Steven Rosen, "Nuclearization and Stability in the Middle East," in Onkar Marwah and Ann Schulz, eds., *Nuclear Proliferation and the Near Nuclear Countries* (Cambridge, Mass.: Ballinger Publishing Co., 1975), p. 159; also Harkavy, "Pariah States," p. 144.

7. Shai Feldman, *Israeli Nuclear Deterrence: A Strategy for the 1980's* (New York: Columbia University Press, 1982.)

8. *Haaretz*, March 15, 1976.

9. *Washington Post*, December 3, 1974.

10. *New York Times*, June 25, 1981.

11. *Africa Contemporary Record*, quoted by Edouard Bustin, "South Africa's Foreign Policy Alternatives and Deterrence Needs," in Marwah and Schulz, *Nuclear Proliferation*, p. 217.

12. United States Central Intelligence Agency, "Prospects for Further Proliferation of Nuclear Weapons," A Memorandum, September 4, 1974. A CIA spokesman later said that the memorandum had been declassified in error and that the agency would refuse any further comment. *Yediot Aharonot*, May 17, 1985.

13. See especially Elaine Davenport, Paul Eddy, and Peter Gillman, *The Plumbat Affair* (London: Futura Publications, 1978); Peter Pry, *Israel's Nuclear Arsenal* (Boulder, Co.: Westview Press, 1984); Spector's above "Proliferation: The Silent Spread" relies on Atomic Energy Commission documents that also mention the reported uranium theft.

14. Robert Manning and Stephen Talbot, "White House Nuclear Report: What's in the Clouds?", *New West*, June 2, 1980, and elsewhere.

15. *Christian Science Monitor*, December 2, 1981.

16. Spector, "Proliferation: The Silent Spread"; James Adams, *The Unnatural Alliance* (London: Quartet Books, 1984), p. 160; *New York Times*, June 25, 1981.

17. Zdenek Cervenka and Barbara Rogers, *The Nuclear Axis: Secret Collaboration Between West Germany and South Africa* (New York: Times Books, 1978), p. 327.

18. For more details about United States and other Western nuclear cooperation with South Africa, see Adams, *The Unnatural Alliance*, pp. 169–74; Cervenka and Rogers, *The Nuclear Axis*, passim.

19. Adams, *The Unnatural Alliance*, p. 170.

20. Ibid., p. 179; *New York Times*, June 28, 1981, citing a United States Defense Intelligence Agency study.

21. *The Encyclopaedia Judaica* (Jerusalem: Keter Publishers, 1972), 4, p. 615.

22. Ernst Bergman, "South Africa and Israel: Different Countries with Common Problems," Johannesburg: South African Institute of International Affairs, 1968.

23. John De St. Jorre, *A House Divided: South Africa's Uncertain Future* (New York: Carnegie Endowment for International Peace, 1977), p. 96.

24. Ibid. The considerable number of similar statements reflect perhaps a "deterrence of uncertainty" policy. Thus former Information and Interior Minister Cornelius Mulder warned that "if we are attacked, no rules apply at all if it comes to a question of our existence. We will use all means at our disposal, whatever they may be. It is true that we have just completed our own pilot plant that uses very advanced technology and that we have major uranium technology." United Nations General Assembly, "Implementation of the Declaration," p. 28.

25. Spector, "Proliferation: The Silent Spread," and elsewhere.

26. Study cited in *New York Times*, June 28, 1981.

27. Robert Manning and Stephen Talbot, "American Cover-up on Israeli Bomb," *The Middle East* (London, June 1980); John Penycat, "Was it the Bomb?" *New African*, June 1980.

28. Quoted in a Washington Office on Africa Educational Fund report, "The September 22, 1979 Mystery Flash: Did South Africa Detonate a Nuclear Bomb?" Washington, D.C., May 1985, p. 16.

29. Pry, *Israel's Nuclear Arsenal*, p. 3.

30. Executive Office of the President, Office of Science and Technology Policy, "Ad Hoc Panel Report on the September 22 Event," July 1980, in

Washington Office on Africa report, "The September 22, 1979 Mystery Flash," p. 5.

31. United Nations General Assembly, "Implementation of the Declaration," p. 33.

32. Manning and Talbot, "American Cover-up."

33. Adams, *The Unnatural Alliance*, pp. 193–95, citing *Aviation Week and Space Technology* and other sources; Jack Anderson in the *Washington Post*, September 16, 1980; "Navy Lab Concludes the Vela Saw a Bomb," *Science*, August 29, 1980.

34. "Navy Lab Concludes the Vela Saw a Bomb," *Science*, August 29, 1980.

35. Manning and Talbot, "American Cover-up"; *Wall Street Journal*, July 16, 1980. According to the aforementioned Washington Office on Africa study and the *Washington Post* reports on which it relies, the search for radioactivity began three weeks later.

36. Penycat, "Was It the Bomb?," p. 36.

37. The report is cited in *Maariv*, February 11, 1981.

38. Adams, *The Unnatural Alliance*, p. 109.

39. Manning and Talbot, "American Cover-up"; Penycat, "Was it the Bomb?"; Washington Office on Africa report, "The September 22, 1979 Mystery Flash," p. 16.

40. Jack Anderson in the *Washington Post*, April 26, 1985.

41. The Washington Office on Africa report, "The September 22, 1979 Mystery Flash," pp. 1–2.

42. Ibid., p. 12.

43. Adams, *The Unnatural Alliance*, p. 195.

44. *Washington Post*, December 8, 1980.

45. Amos Perlmutter et al., *Two Minutes Over Bagdad* (London: Vallentine, Mitchell & Co., 1982).

46. Ibid., pp. 50–51.

47. Hirsh Goodman, "The Star Wars Opportunity," *Jerusalem Post* International Edition, April 20, 1985.

CHAPTER 8

"Everyone Does It": The Question of Double Standards

South Africa is the only country with which we maintain relations where our main problem is not so much that of explaining Israel and her positions with the aim of improving those relations but rather that of maintaining a low profile on what are embarrassingly good relations.

—A senior Israeli diplomat, as quoted by Yosef Goell in *Africa Report*, Nov.–Dec. 1980

The evidence reviewed in previous chapters cannot leave much doubt about the material and psychological importance of the Israeli connection to South Africa's leaders. The suggestion that Israel is an important ally of South Africa, however, does not suit Israeli representatives and others who defend Israeli policies in the West, such as major American Jewish organizations. As the following examples show, the arguments these spokesmen have offered in rebuttal over the years amount to the following:

1. Ties with South Africa do not imply approval of apartheid, and Israel has repeatedly said it opposes all sorts of racism. Recall, for instance, the refusal of the Israeli Ambassador I. Unna to attend the premiere of the play *Golda* in a segregated Pretoria theater in 1978.[1]

2. What collaboration with South Africa? There may be various unproven rumors and PLO-inspired propaganda aimed at delegitimizing Israel, but the truth is, and International Monetary Fund (IMF) figures prove it, that Israeli trade with South Africa is miniscule. Besides, the South African Jewish community has been a major consideration for Israel. (As recently

as mid-1985, Michael Curtis of the very partisan "American Professors for Peace in the Middle East" stated, without as much as acknowledging the existence of James Adams' book, that "Israel and South Africa are not allies and no entente cordiale exists between them." It is a "distortion," he wrote, to depict Israel as "a close associate of South Africa.")[2]

3. So Israel does have certain ties with South Africa, but everybody "does it." Why single out Israel?

It is not immediately obvious that questions of "fairness to Israel" and "double standards" belong in a monograph such as this, which does not have among its goals the assigning or reassigning of blame. Such a defense would probably work for no other country: If a supporter of the British government attempted to block discussion of British–South African ties with the argument that France and West Germany do it too, the attempt would no doubt be dismissed with contempt. But allegations of this sort preoccupy so many writers on the South African–Israeli relationship and constitute such a large portion of the published wisdom on this subject that it becomes appropriate to address them directly. In such writings the entire question of Israeli–South African ties is often treated as artificial, if not illegitimate, a creation of Israel's enemies.

Israel does say it opposes racism. Israeli officials have taken verbal issue with South African apartheid on numerous occasions. But so have most friends and supporters of the Pretoria government. And, if verbal opposition is the yardstick, even President P. W. Botha is no fan of apartheid, judging by his statements about the need to transcend the "outmoded" system of apartheid. Opposition to apartheid is universal—and comes dirt cheap. This is well understood by friends of the white minority government such as the Reverend Jerry Falwell, head of the Liberty Federation, formerly the "Moral Majority"; in 1985, as he was campaigning for *reinvestment* in South Africa, he also stated, "I don't believe any Christian could support segregation, apartheid."[3] Substitute "Jew" for "Christian" and nearly identical statements have been issued by Israeli officials as they were authorizing increased cooperation with Pretoria and Israel was boycotting every UN vote on South Africa (see Appendix B).

The assertion about Israel's "miniscule dealings" with South Africa (with IMF figures as evidence) can only be dismissed as fraudulent, as are other versions that acknowledge a fraction of the evidence on the extent of South African–Israeli ties, ignore or dismiss the rest, and proceed to talk about PLO propaganda and anti-Semitism.

Still, is Israel being singled out? Is there a double standard? New York City Mayor Edward Koch certainly thinks so, and it seems safe to say that the way he makes the case is typical: " . . . my response is that it is no more immoral for Israel to trade with South Africa than it is for other nations, Great Britain, the United States, and others to do so. The same standards and the same loud denunciations do not seem to apply to other nations. Why not?"[4]

(Note the focus on trade—civilian trade, that is.) Mayor Koch can even see himself some day joining those who ask Israel to stop trading with South Africa, but a few things would have to happen first:

When the nations of black Africa reestablish diplomatic relationships with Israel, end their economic boycott against it, rescind the abominable "Zionism is racism" resolution and put their own countries on the line in the struggle for freedom inside South Africa, then—and only then—those of us who support the suffering citizens of South Africa will join in asking Israel to cut its ties and cut off all trade with the nation.

Moshe Decter, who, in response to criticism of Israeli ties with South Africa in the 1970s, prepared reports for the American Jewish Congress showing the extent of Western and African ties with Pretoria, did not leave the matter unexplained:

First, many of the [UN] committee members do business with the Western states and the U.S.S.R. Out of their own interests, it would not do to criticize or condemn these countries for maintaining a massive arms traffic and other commerce with South Africa. It is far easier to find a suitable scapegoat.
Second, focusing the world's attention on Israel's trade with South Africa helps to distract attention from their own culpability.
Finally, anti-Semitism continues to operate as an irrational combination of unreasoning ignorance and wild prejudice.[5]

South Africa indeed owes much of its economic and military might to loans, massive investments, diplomatic support, and arms supplies from the Western powers. These powers readily accepted Pretoria's claims that it is a "strategic asset" for Western defense, making the land of apartheid an important market for weapons as its disenfranchised population served as a source of inexpensive labor. The great majority of foreign investment in South Africa comes, in descending order, from Britain, the United States, West Germany, France and Switzerland. At the UN, the West has repeatedly opposed attempts to impose tough international sanctions against Pretoria.[6]

The United States is South Africa's largest single trading partner. In 1985 this trade amounted to $3.38 billion; Common Market trade with South Africa amounted to $10.3 billion. According to 1985 figures of the United States Department of Commerce, some $8 billion worth of shares of South African companies were being held in the United States; loans to South Africa amounted to $3.5 billion.[7] Until General Motors, IBM, and other major companies began to sell their assets in South Africa in the mid-1980s, American companies dominated the South African computer industry and played a central role in other vital industries such as petroleum (45 percent) and automobiles (30 percent). Advocating disinvestment is a criminal offense in South Africa.

Under "constructive engagement," the policy of the U.S. government through most of the Reagan era, Pretoria continued to be treated as an ally, albeit one that had to be encouraged with friendly persuasion to make some internal changes. The President campaigned against sanctions until the last minute, and then reluctantly accepted relatively mild veto-proof packages legislated by Congress in 1985 and again in 1986. "Constructive engagement" was described by John Conyers, a Congressional critic, as "protesting apartheid with one hand while feeding it with the other."[8] It was, he went on, a "toothless euphemism disguising military, economic and diplomatic support for Pretoria." According to a study the Congressman prepared, the United States government has also lifted restrictions on exporting police and military equipment to South Africa; "dual use" equipment, ostensibly for civilian use but in reality used by the South African army and police, was similarly permitted. This made it possible for South Africa to obtain police aircraft, electric shock batons, military and space electronics, computers, optical guidance equipment, as well as arms manufacturing technology.[9]

Black African countries have also found themselves among South Africa's business partners, often due to the *force majeure* of history and imperialism. The dependence of some African nations on employment and trade with South Africa may qualify as "one of the most glaring instances of the exploitative imperial-colonial legacy"; consequently, "the effort of these states to transform, indeed negate this relationship is the very essence of the independence period." [10] One such glaring example is Lesotho, a former British High Commission territory which is fully surrounded by South Africa. In the mid-1980s, about half of Lesotho's labor force was being employed in South Africa. The currency of Lesotho is the South African rand. The two countries also share a costly hydroelectric system. Due to geography and transportation constraints, most of Zimbabwe's imports and exports pass through South African ports, as do most of Zambia's exports.

Oil from the Middle East has found its way to South Africa, in most cases through Western middlemen. Saudi and Kuwaiti officials say their countries observe the oil embargo and cannot control what oil companies or other traders later do with the oil. The destination of a shipment is often unknown when the oil is loaded. Still, although they do not condone it, oil-exporting countries have not gone out of their way to adopt the most stringent measures to prevent shipments to South Africa. The "How-about-Arab-oil-to-South-Africa" theme seems to have become a favorite with Israeli spokesmen, second only to the citing of IMF figures.

Clearly, dozens of countries, including even some in Eastern Europe, can be found somewhere or other on the long list of Pretoria's trading partners. And, as Israeli officials gleefully point out, Western European companies are still guilty of occasional violations of the arms embargo; it is also true that the governments of these countries sometimes turn a blind eye to the violations.

But military relations between South Africa and the West are no longer nearly as warm as they used to be. At present only Israel can boast a systematic government-to-government arms relationship with Pretoria: "It is clear that the embargo has severely restricted the ability of South Africa to purchase major arms systems. Israel is now the only avenue they can turn to," concluded Joseph Hanlon, the British expert on sanctions and author of *The Sanctions Handbook*. (Interview in the *Jerusalem Post*, March 27, 1987). Whatever embargo violations Western European countries are guilty of, "none do so on Israel's scale," he pointed out. "Israel is already the worst offender—and the main conduit for dealers breaking the arms embargo—and everyone assumes that it will continue to be," in all probability even after the forced "no additional military contracts" Israeli announcement in March 1987.

As the arms relationship between South Africa and the West began to cool off in the 1970s and Pretoria was forced to build its own arms industry, Israel stepped in to fill the gaps in hardware and technology. ARMSCOR, the Armaments Corporation of South Africa, became a success in no small measure due to the partnership with Israel. Technology transfers and joint weapons development, it should be recalled, are much harder to come by than hardware, many types of which are readily available on the international arms market. The Israeli readiness to share its military tactics and counterinsurgency expertise with South African troops is another unique contribution. And no Western country is now known to cooperate with South Africa on nuclear weapons, as Israel almost certainly does.

Since the early 1970s, whenever South African leaders would ask themselves who were their friends in this hostile world, they had good reason to look up to Israel. It was Israel that boycotted nearly all anti-apartheid United Nations votes; Israel was willing to enter into joint military and economic ventures, offering itself as a springboard for South African exports to the EEC and the United States. Establishment Israelis have dealt with the Bantustans and their leaders; other South African dignitaries have been received in Israel with levels of hospitality that would be unthinkable elsewhere in the West and indeed in most of the rest of the world (chapter 10). And if the West should impose tougher sanctions against Pretoria, it will be surprising indeed if reports about Israel's serving as a secret lifeline do not begin to come shortly afterwards.

John F. Burns of the *New York Times* reported the following in 1977, but the same could have been said at any time since, and can still be said today:

Most whites here celebrate the growth of the relationship [with Israel] over the last three years. It has given South Africa access to armaments that are increasingly difficult to get elsewhere as well as opening healthy trade in other items. Moreover, it has offered South Africa diplomatic comfort at a time when its old friends in the West have become increasingly alienated by apartheid.[11]

Within Israel, one finds considerably more openness and candor about the ties with South Africa than among supporters in the West, as is often true regarding other issues. Thus in 1985 as these supporters were busy churning out tracts about "miniscule trade" and double standards in singling out Israel, liberal Knesset Member Yossi Sarid of the Citizens Rights Movement observed: "Some countries have consorted with South Africa in dark alleys. Israel has been the only country to walk with South Africa on Main Street of its own volition. The romance was so heated that we were even willing to have an illicit affair with the lady's despicable daughters: Ciskei and Transkei. . . . It was a nauseating act of prostitution." [12]

NOTES

1. Michael Curtis, "Israel and South Africa," *Middle East Review* Special Report, October 1983; Leslie D. Simon, "Israel and South Africa: The Allegations and the Reality," Institute for Jewish Policy Planning and Research of the Synagogue Council of America, 1980.

2. Michael Curtis, "Africa, Israel and the Middle East," *Middle East Review*, Summer 1985. For another example see Leonard J. Davis, *Myths and Facts: A Concise Record of the Arab-Israeli Conflict* (Washington, D.C.: Near East Research, 1985), p. 15.

3. *New York Times*, August 22, 1985, p. 10.

4. *Jewish Press*, January 18, 1985.

5. Moshe Decter, "The Arms Traffic with South Africa: Who is Guilty?" The American Jewish Congress, New York, 1976.

6. For further details about Western–South African relations and cooperation, see for instance, Kunirum Osia, *Israel, South Africa and Black Africa* (New York: University Press of America, 1981), pp. 35–92, and sources.

7. Figures cited in *Newsday*, April 14, 1985.

8. Op-ed page in *New York Times*, January 23, 1985.

9. Findings reported by James Ridgeway, "Reagan's Secret Aid to Apartheid," *Village Voice*, December 25, 1984.

10. Richard Stevens and Abdelwahab M. Elmessiri, *Israel and South Africa: The Progression of a Relationship* (New York: New World Press, 1976), p. 1.

11. John F. Burns, "South Africa Gains Arms and Trade as Israel Link Hardens," *New York Times*, May 21, 1977.

12. *Haaretz*, October 24, 1985.

CHAPTER 9

South African Jews: Is Silence Golden?

South African Jewry is largely an upper-middle-class community, which at the time of the 1980 census numbered less than 118,000 out of a population of some 30 million. Most Jews arrived from eastern Europe between the 1880s and World War II. Today about 60 percent live in the Johannesburg area and another 20 percent in Cape Town.[1] The community has made a disproportionately high contribution to South Africa's economy and culture. Jews were prominent in the emerging gold and diamond industries as well as in clothing, furniture, and food. Today they are also well represented in finance, industry, medicine, and law.

The anti-Semitic record of the National Party and its opposition to Jewish immigration before it took office in 1948 were already discussed in chapter 2. All this opposition changed abruptly in 1948 when the white authorities recognized the wisdom of seeking better relations with the white, prosperous Jewish community. Given the short supply of South Africans with white pigmentation, it was only natural for Prime Minister Daniel Malan to announce that the government would not support discrimination against "any segment of the white population."[2]

That government promise has been kept. The community found itself in the unique situation of being under a Christian government that subjected the majority population to severe repression and discrimination but held the Jews in favor. A 1985 American Jewish Committee report found "virtually no trace of any discrimination."[3] The "white" classification has enabled South African Jews to get elected to the Parliament and Senate and to become mayors.[4] (There are, however, anti-Semitic Afrikaner groups on the extreme right, especially the Herstigte Nasionale Party and the Afrikaner Resistance Movement).

Jewish immigration to Israel has been proportionately higher from South Africa than from any other Western country.[5] (Percentages aside, that is not to say that Israeli officials are satisfied. Even when South Africa was in deep crisis in 1985–1986, all but a relative handful of the Jews who emigrated preferred to go to the West.) In a typical year, according to South African–born Roy Isacowitz of the *Jerusalem Post*, about 500 South African Jews would move to Israel but less than one third of them would stay.[6] Atypical years with large increases were those after the Sharpeville and Soweto shootings.

A number of prominent Israelis are South African–born: former Foreign Minister Abba Eban; Samuel Katz, the right-wing publisher and former advisor to Prime Minister Begin; Michael Comay, who represented Israel at the United Nations; and the late Louis Aryeh Pincus, former chairman of the Jewish Agency Executive.

In recent decades tens of thousands of Jews have emigrated to South Africa—from Israel. Their number, including those there under security contracts, is currently estimated at 25,000.[7] This is the largest source of postwar Jewish emigration to South Africa. Many of these emigrants evidently decided that there is no future for them in Israel, but there is one in South Africa. One Johannesburg housing development is said to have signs enforcing apartheid in Hebrew.

The South African Jewish community is known for its generous contributions to Israel, the highest amount per capita of any Jewish community in the world. (It holds a similar record for involvement in Zionist organizations.) The white authorities have been unusually cooperative by exempting Israel from the severe restrictions on currency transfers abroad. These restrictions would have barred similar transfers to the United States or Britain, for instance. Israel is also the only country permitted to sell its government bonds in South Africa.

Some in the West believe, apparently less on the basis of fact than of wishful thinking, that most South African Jews are active in or supportive of anti-apartheid causes. Many in the forefront of opposition to apartheid are indeed Jewish, most notably Helen Suzman (who is vehemently opposed to divestment), and others mentioned later. Jews for Social Justice in Johannesburg and Jews for Justice in Cape Town, as well as Jewish student organizations such as the South African Union of Jewish Students, are known for their anti-apartheid stance. But the community as a whole, it should be recalled, is a segment of the white population. Its leaders are opposed to sanctions and favor continued economic, cultural, and tourist ties with Israel. They have no desire to risk a revival of white anti-Semitism. Certainly not very many South African Jews wish to see majority rule and another Rhodesia.[8] At the same time, they would like to avoid antagonizing the African majority, a situation sometimes described as a "tightrope," "painful dilemma," etc.

Not only has there been no large-scale Jewish political activism against white privilege or hostile criticism of the government, Jewish participation in the National Party and in establishment organizations has been increasing.[9] This statement too needs to be qualified: There is no widespread enthusiasm for the goals and policies of the National Party; districts with a large Jewish population often vote for Suzman's Progressive Federal Party (PFP). But, to make matters more complicated still, it is often said caustically in South Africa that the automatic vote many Jews cast for the PFP does not keep them from praying that the party never comes to power.

There are two major South African Jewish organizations: The South African Jewish Board of Deputies, which deals primarily with domestic matters, and the South African Zionist Federation, concerned with the promotion of Zionism, immigration, and ties with Israel. The Board of Deputies, established in 1903 after the South African War, serves as an umbrella for the approximately 320 Jewish organizations affiliated with it, and as such is very nearly the official spokesman for the entire Jewish community.

For the first eighty years or so of its existence, the board did not regard racial segregation as one of the domestic matters to speak out on. The reasoning was that the South African Jewish organization was a "non-political body which refrains from taking any position on party political issues and does not express views on the various race policies being advocated."[10] About the farthest the board went in the 1960s and 1970s was to call for "harmonious relations" between all groups of the South African population. Although in the early 1960s the organization managed to issue a statement critical of Israel's anti–South African stance at the UN, it had nothing to say after the Sharpeville massacre.[11]

The policy of speaking up against discrimination only when Jews were the targets made sense to South African Jewish writer Dan Jacobson. In an exchange with a critic in *Commentary* he explained:

Each group must act in defense of what it perceives to be its own interests or else it ceases to exist as a group. . . . It is impossible for me to imagine that any community will ever sacrifice itself for the sake of another. . . . The martyrdom and self sacrifices that he calls for from the entire community appear on the whole to be gratuitous, disinterested.[12]

At stake was, as another writer pointed out sympathetically, "a standard of life far better than they could obtain anywhere else. There is a plentitude of sunshine and servants"; if there was any guilt, it was eased "by extra kindness and consideration of their African servants and employees."[13] (This might be described as an improvement since the 1950s when Dan Jacobson had observed that "*Die schwarze*/the Blacks are talked of as contemptuously at Jewish tea parties as they are at gatherings of English and Afrikaans-speaking whites.")[14]

There are no Jewish counterparts to world-famous, anti-apartheid, Christian clergymen such as Desmond Tutu and Allan Boesak. After Dr. Hendrik Verwoerd's death in 1966, Chief Rabbi Bernard Casper of Johannesburg, speaking before an overflow crowd, described the architect of apartheid as someone who is "in true scriptural sense a man of valour."[15] In Cape Town, the Chief Rabbi eulogized Verwoerd as "a man of sincerity and deep integrity. . . . A moral conscience underlay his policies. He was the first man to give apartheid a moral ground."[16] And at the Progressive Jewish Congregation the Rabbi mourned the death of "one of the greatest, if not the greatest Prime Ministers South Africa has ever produced . . . who like Moses of old, had led his people through the promised land after 60 years of wandering. . . ."[17]

Of course not all Jews felt this way. As the Board of Deputies continued to talk about apartheid as a "political" issue on which there can be no "collective Jewish position," prominent Jews organized to oppose a system in which there was such a striking link between white prosperity on the one hand and black exploitation and misery on the other. Some Jews were perhaps reminded of the Nuremberg Laws and other dark periods in Jewish history. Among these leaders were Ellen Hellmann, a leading figure in the Institute of Race Relations and a member of the Board of Deputies; Israel Maisels, defense counsel in the great Treason Trial; and Harold Hanson, who was one of the founders of the Liberal Party. And then there was the diminutive South African Communist Party, the only party that was open to blacks; it did not get many Jewish votes, but Jews were overrepresented in its leadership.

In effect, all Jewish anti-apartheid dissenters were conforming to the policy of the Board of Deputies: individuals may do what they wish, but there is no collective position. That, at least, was the official stance. The actual preference of the board may have been somewhat different, at least judging by former Senator Leslie Rubin's testimony that the board was in fact taking a dim view of even private opposition to the South African government. "I was told more than once while in Parliament," he recalled, "that my prominence as a critic of apartheid and a spokesman for the African people was an embarrassment to the Board of Deputies. Other Jews experienced similar attempts to persuade them to tone down their opposition to the government." [18] But then, it should also be mentioned that the board refused to go on record as identifying with the "struggle for survival" of the Afrikaner, an idea proposed by journalist Henry Katzew. [19]

In recent years the board has begun to pay attention to Jewish criticism and pleas from abroad. South African Jews had long been urged to cease being, as one American observer put it, "non-political, law-abiding patriotic bystanders silent in the face of evil." [20] Recent board resolutions have made references to the need to remove discriminatory legislation in South Africa; in 1982 the board also expressed opposition to detention without trial. At this writing the most far-reaching resolution is the one adopted in 1985 after calls from the World Jewish Congress and three days of debates. [21] That resolution favors "the removal of all provisions in the laws of South Africa which discriminate on grounds of color and race." All concerned are asked to "do everything possible to insure the establishment of a climate of peace and calm in which dialogue, negotiation and processes of reform can be continued." A concurrent resolution expressed solidarity with Israel. (Whether the above goes much beyond what the National Party itself claims to stand for is debatable.)

Later Dr. Israel Abramowitz, president of B'nai Brith in South Africa and former chairman of the Board of Deputies, reminded an audience that the future of the South African Jewish community is tied with that of the whites. South African Jews, he said, find an "obsessional preoccupation" with their country in the United States. These troublesome protests have a "purely American political motivation." [22]

In late 1986 the Union of Orthodox Jewish Congregations (United States) passed a resolution that was as mild as can be imagined, calling upon Jewish organizations and individuals to refrain from stock ownership in those companies that still failed to follow the non-discriminatory Sullivan principles in their South African operations. That, however, was too much for Chief Rabbi Casper of Johannesburg who promptly wrote to express his "amazement" at the resolution, which "cannot be to the benefit of our community" and "caused me and my honoured colleagues considerable embarrassment." [23]

The subject of South African Jewry may be of interest, but how relevant is it to understanding the South African-Israeli relationship? Not much, it would seem from the evidence, the insistence of Israeli spokesmen to the contrary notwithstanding. That South African Jews are somehow a decisive factor in the Pretoria-Jerusalem embrace has become an article of faith for many others in the West, but it remains an unexamined and unproven assertion. To believe that South African Jews are "a major factor" is to believe that the ties between the governments would not be what they are now if, say, there were no Jews in South Africa or if they all emigrated. But precisely what would be different, and how? Would 35 percent of Israel's military exports not have gone to South Africa? Would there be no Israeli scientists at South African nuclear facilities? Would officials not have offered Israel as a way station for South African products to Western markets? Have South African Jews requested any or all of the above?

Israel and South Africa, it should be clear by now, have plenty of material reasons to be allies, and the next two chapters will suggest still more factors. Still, can it not be argued that Israel has no choice but to maintain decent relations with Pretoria because of its concern for this important community? Certainly it can be argued, and Israeli officials have done so repeatedly. (The argument was also used to justify Israeli arms sales to Iran, the junta in Argentina, and elsewhere.) But consider the following: When it was in Israel's interest to vote against South Africa at the United Nations in the 1960s, it did so. The whites—and even the Board of Deputies—were furious, but concern for South African Jews was not the compelling consideration.

Similarly, Israeli concern for the much larger Soviet Jewish community did not stop the government from taking steps that it judged in Israel's interest, such as strategic cooperation with the United States, participation in the "Star Wars" scheme, or accepting a powerful Voice of America transmitter. When Israeli advisers trained South African forces in counterinsurgency tactics, no one in Israel suggested that, for the sake of Soviet Jews, similar advisers be offered to the Soviets in Afghanistan.

It is furthermore clear that the future of the white-minority regime is far from bright. How being an ally of such a government can help the interests of South African Jews, especially in the long run, has not been explained by any Israeli official. There is now a measure of skepticism even in the Israeli press about government claims that its South African policy is dictated by concern for the Jewish community; one example is an August 21, 1986 editorial in the right-of-center *Maariv*, which expressed concern that Western sanctions against South Africa might force Israel to make decisions "we would all rather avoid making," and then "the claim that all this [business with Pretoria] is being done in order to insure the welfare of the Jewish community in South Africa will no longer sound that convincing."

In March of 1987, the Israeli government, fearing a reduction in U.S. military aid, announced that it would not sign additional military contracts with South Africa. South African Jewish leaders, as well as government officials in Pretoria, expressed understanding for Israel's predicament (see epilogue). South African Jews did not seem to be much of a factor in the Israeli announcement, nor did Pretoria retaliate against them once the announcement was made. South African Jews have been more of an alibi than an explanation for what Jerusalem and Pretoria have done together.

NOTES

1. David Geller, "The Jewish Community of South Africa," A Background Memorandum, The International Relations Department of the American Jewish Committee, New York, May 1985, p. 1.

2. Henry Katzew, "Jews in the Land of Apartheid," *Midstream*, December 1962.

3. Geller, "The Jewish Community," p. 2.

4. *American Jewish Yearbook*, 1972, p. 581.

5. Geller, "The Jewish Community," p. 1.

6. Roy Isacowitz, "A Tale of Two Loyalties," *Jerusalem Post* International Edition, January 4, 1986, p. 13. Somewhat different figures can be found in South Africa's *Jewish Affairs*, December 1985, pp. 67–68.

7. James Adams, *The Unnatural Alliance* (London: Quartet Books, 1984), p. 7; Also Geller, "The Jewish Community," p. 1.

8. On South African Jewry's stance towards apartheid, see, for instance, "South Africa, Its Jews and the Israeli Connection" by Marcus Arkin, director of the South African Zionist Federation, writing in *South Africa International*, October 1977; Robert G. Weisbord, "The Dilemma of South African Jewry," *Journal of Modern African Studies*, No. 2, 1967; E. Feit, "Community in a Quandary: The South African Jewish Community and Apartheid," *Race* 8 (4) April 1967; Kunirum Osia, *Israel, South Africa and Black Africa* (New York: University Press of America, 1981), pp. 5–15, quoting from and citing a variety of sources.

9. Arkin, "South Africa, Its Jews, and the Israeli Connection."

10. Cited by Richard Stevens in "Zionism, South Africa and Apartheid: The Paradoxical Triangle," *Phylon*, no. 2, Summer 1971.

11. For a detailed discussion, see Katzew's article "Jews in the Land of Apartheid."

12. Dan Jacobson and Ronald Segal, "Apartheid and South African Jewry: An Exchange," *Commentary*, November 1957.

13. Feit, "Community in a Quandary," p. 408.

14. Dan Jacobson, "The Jews of South Africa: Portrait of a Flourishing Community," *Commentary*, January 1957, p. 44.

15. Osia, *Israel, South Africa and Black Africa*, p. 19, citing the *Rand Daily Mail*.

16. Ibid.

17. Ibid.

18. Leslie Rubin, "Dialog: South African Jewry and Apartheid," *Africa Report*, February 1970, p. 24.

19. Gideon Shimoni, *Jews and Zionism: The South African Experience 1910–1967* (Cape Town: Oxford University Press, 1980), p. 293.

20. Weisbord, "The Dilemma of South African Jewry," p. 241.

21. World Jewish Congress, "South African Jews Reject Apartheid," A Memorandum, June 12, 1985.

22. *Jewish Press*, July 19, 1985, p. 1.

23. *Jewish Press*, December 19, 1986, p. 2; January 2, 1987, p. 1.

CHAPTER 10

Open Arms and Red Carpets

Most of the preceding material dealt with transactions that are directly associated with the pursuit of better military, economic, and political standing. There is nothing surprising or unusual in any of this; it is what governments are there for. Moral considerations and principles are not what international politics is about. States do not often pass up profitable transactions solely because of the political character of their partners; even embargoes might not prove more than a minor inconvenience.

If the relationship is between governments whose ideologies are or appear to be dissimilar, it is said that politics makes strange bedfellows, unnatural alliances. The virtually uninterrupted Israeli weapons sales to Iran, both under the Shah and Khomeini, are a case in point; since 1985 it has been reported that even Beijing, which does not have diplomatic relations with Jerusalem, was interested in more extensive commercial, and possibly military, ties with Israel.[1]

Can Israeli ties with South Africa be fully explained as another example of realpolitik practiced by two relatively isolated states with few alternatives? Did the harsh realities of this world require Israel to make a painful sacrifice and deal reluctantly with the white minority government? The official Israeli stance parallels some of the above realpolitik arguments. (In most cases spokesmen also insist the ties are ''normal'' and not particularly close.) For instance, after noting that Israel opposes apartheid, former Assistant Director of the Israeli Ministry of Foreign Affairs Yaakov Shimoni explained:

our international relations are based, like those of most countries in the world, on the assumption that countries maintain normal relations between existing governments whether you like the government or you dislike it . . . I do not know how many of the 145 members of the United Nations you could have relations with if you had relations only with those countries whose regimes you like, which you think are just fine . . . [In addition] we have the specific problem of a fairly large Jewish community. We feel a certain pang of responsibility for them[2]

But Israeli–South African relations do not look at all like those we would expect between reluctant bedfellows with nothing in common but interests. White South Africans closely identify with Israel and have missed few opportunities to show their admiration and empathy. Numerous establishment Israelis have likewise shown empathy, understanding, and amity towards the besieged white minority. Manifestations such as red carpet receptions for South African officials, establishment by Knesset members of a friendship league with South Africa, or attendance by members at ceremonies for Bantustan leaders, twin city agreements and the like should call into question the belief that the relationship is only about vital transactions between partners indifferent to each other. This chapter reviews some of these less quantifiable aspects of the Israeli–South African relationship. The next chapter proposes why South Africa and Israel are not, and do not act like, strange bedfellows.

Afrikaners have long noticed that their struggle for survival at the foot of Africa parallels that of another "white" country near the head of the continent:

With the partition of Palestine and the establishment of Israel, an apartheid was at the same time carried into effect which had the result that hundreds of thousands of Arab refugees from the Jewish area languished in neighbouring Arab states and formed an insoluble international problem. We say this with no reproach. But Israel owes its existence to the refusal of its Jewish citizens to accept integration and equality with an Arab majority in one state. The apartheid policy is based on the same attitude by European South Africans toward the non-European majority.[3]

Since the countries were seen as sharing a common lot, "their community of interests had better be utilized than denied" (chapter 2). South Africa supported Israel in all its wars, and the Israeli victories were a source of inspiration. Among those who felt aroused was General H. van den Berghe, former head of the South African Bureau of

State Security (BOSS): "I went to Israel recently and enjoyed every moment there. I told the Prime Minister when I got back that as long as Israel exists we have hope."[4] Excitement about Israel is not limited to the South African leadership: In one Markinor survey, respondents ranked their favorite countries and Israel was at the top.[5] There are also numerous "Christian Action for Israel" groups.

Invasions and destabilization of neighboring countries to combat "terrorism" ring a familiar bell in South Africa and are often equated with similar Israeli actions that were met with more understanding in the West. (Thus Israel is admired not only for its military adventures and victories, but also for managing to retain a generally favorable image in the West in the process.) After a trip to South Africa, *New York Times* columnist Flora Lewis observed that "comparison with Israel has become an insistent theme in South Africa when people there discuss their country's actions." For instance, "after the murderous South African raid on Lesotho recently, an American correspondent asked the Foreign Ministry how it explained talks with Angola one day and an armed attack on a neighbor next. The answer was simply that Israel invaded Lebanon while negotiating with Egypt and this has been accepted." The African National Congress was regularly equated with the PLO; some in South Africa spoke of "Menachem Botha" and "Magnus Sharon."[6]

The pattern is different in Israel: leaders and the mass media do not regularly equate Israel's history and present problems with those of South Africa. Few Israelis would agree or appreciate hearing that their country is in the same boat as South Africa, although some of those concerned about birth rates on the occupied West Bank fear "another South Africa." But while it is true that there has been little outspoken support and admiration for Pretoria in Israel, it is also true that when it comes to showing amity and cordiality towards South African representatives, Israel has often gone well beyond other countries, Western and non-Western. Consider P. W. Botha's tour of Western Europe in the summer of 1984. In Germany,

A large upholstered sofa was removed from West German Chancellor Helmut Kohl's office last week minutes before South Africa's Prime Minister P. W. Botha came to call. The Chancellor typically sits on the sofa with his foreign guests as photographers snap. This time, Mr. Kohl stared unsmilingly and stiff next to a relaxed-looking Mr. Botha. The Chancellor declined to re-enact a handshake for the cameramen, who did, however immortalize the departing piece of furniture.[7]

In London, Botha's presence "detonated a huge demonstration" and "photographs of her [Margaret Thatcher] glowering countenance in pictures with Mr. Botha were meant to convey Britain's disapproval of apartheid."

Israeli leaders, by contrast, seem to believe that that is no way to treat a white guest from South Africa. Several months later, in November, Foreign Minister Roelof Botha came to Jerusalem. Israeli Foreign Minister Izhak Shamir had to have a state-level reception and "went to Ben-Gurion airport, rolled a red carpet in front of the guest, received him according to all the rules of protocol and even invited reporters to photograph his meeting with Botha at the Foreign Ministry."[8] (An Associated Press photo showed Botha and Shamir beaming and shaking hands). Botha also met with Defense Minister Rabin, was driven in an official limousine and served a state dinner. *Maariv* columnist Amnon Abramowitz observed that other countries in the West may do business with South Africa "quietly under the table," but Israel's approach is reminiscent of the Jew who not only eats pork but also drips grease for everyone to see.

Israel's reception of Botha was not an aberration. Recall the way Vorster was received in 1976 by a Labor government. Or, the treatment extended to South African Treasury Minister Owen Horwood by Prime Minister Menachem Begin and other officials in December of 1980. The guest was invited to a reception in a Yeshiva, attended by Chief Rabbi Ovadia Yosef and Jerusalem Mayor Teddy Kolek; Rabbi Yosef wished the South African well, saying, "may all the Torah's blessings come true for you."[9] Igal Horowitz, Horwood's Israeli counterpart, praised the "deep ties" between Israel and South Africa without even the most perfunctory condemnation of apartheid. The South African journal *Beeld* reported that the Hebrew University in Jerusalem awarded Horwood an honorary doctorate in philosophy.[10] "This is not part of a normal relationship which we have to have," complained Knesset member Amnon Rubinstein who does favor "normal" relations with South Africa. "This is blatant disregard for the basic sensitivity we must have as Jews and Israelis." As soon as people arrive in South Africa, Rubinstein went on, they are reminded of the ghetto, of the Pale, of stamps in identity cards and of places that

are off-limits in a country where the most elementary rights are denied
and dissent is suppressed. The Knesset critic also noted that by Pretoria's standards most of today's Israelis might be classified as non-
whites. Some Israelis have in fact been "mistakenly" abused or removed from "white" buses.[11]

None of these problems stopped General Nathan Nir, chairman of
the Israeli Association for the Welfare of Soldiers from visiting South
Africa the following year "on a mission to help give soldiers the feeling that they are needed and appreciated." Naturally, he also met—
"privately"—with several high-ranking military officers and praised
the raid into Angola as the only way to deal with terrorists who must
be "attacked at their bases. In this way they would never feel safe."[12]

It is not uncommon for Israelis or the Israeli media to refer to those
who resist apartheid as "terrorists," by which South Africa, like Israel, is plagued. (To tell whether such characterizations are the norm
would require further research.) Similarly, Pretoria's perspective on
events in Southern Africa has been adopted by Israeli state and private
media at least some of the time: Israeli television viewers were treated
by the state-run network to a South African program celebrating the
"new state of Transkei"; resistance in Soweto was explained as
"criminal violence" perpetrated by "Communist elements and outside
agitators"; and some newspapers described American diplomatic initiatives in Southern Africa as a "sellout" of the kind that Israel might
expect.[13]

Looking at the Knesset record in the 1970s and early to mid-1980s,
one finds that the legislative body has had very little to say about
Israel's "second most important ally after the United States." The
topic came up for debate perhaps once or twice in all those years.
What protest there has been in the Knesset or the media was less likely
to focus on being an ally of South Africa than on the failure to avoid
gratuitous visibility and public relations headaches. Thus Shlomo Avineri, former director-general of the Ministry of Foreign Affairs who is
considered a critic of government policy towards South Africa, would
like Israel to "do business with it [South Africa] when it is in our
interest but take care not to appear as condoning by overt acts the
policies of the government."[14]

The great majority of the Israeli public has shown no measurable
concern or opposition. Ties with South Africa burgeoned while being
a non-issue for most Israelis. In general, steps taken by the govern-

ment for the sake of "security" are rarely questioned. Other than a small number of individuals committed to leftist causes, such as "Israelis Against Apartheid," there is no record of demonstrations or sit-ins demanding that ties be cut off. (There are also sporadic reports about small groups forming on the right to press for *warmer* ties with Pretoria, for example, the *Jerusalem Post*, August 28, 1985.)

Developments that would be met with vehement protests and boycotts in the United States or Western Europe often pass without notice in Israel; financial considerations have prevailed in situations where most other Western governments or even private companies would likely have drawn the line. Thus it is impossible to imagine New York City's Bloomingdale's department store holding a promotional "South Africa Week," as did the Shalom department store in Tel Aviv. The event was organized by the South African Department of Commerce with "contributions by the Department of Information in cooperation with the management of Shalom stores." Shoppers were offered "information" about South Africa as a bonus.[15] A similar "South Africa Week" was held by Supersol, the largest Israeli supermarket chain.[16] Such promotions are common. ("It is sufficient to enter an Israeli supermarket," Naomi Chazan noted in *African Affairs* in 1983, "to see the extent of South African goods.") In Israel, a "made in South Africa" label does not cause too many eyebrows to rise.

South Africa was reportedly the first country to open a state-run tourist office in Israel, in 1979.[17] Four years later Israeli Minister of Tourism Sharir awarded South African Airways the title of "Most Favoured Tourist Undertaking for 1983" for its contribution to the promotion of tourism in Israel.[18] South Africa has been a popular vacation spot for Israelis: Small Israel is now South Africa's fourth largest source of tourists, topped only by England, Germany and the U.S. Israel was also the only country from which tourism to South Africa rose in 1986. By January 21, 1987, when these facts were reported in the *Jerusalem Post*, all flights to South Africa for the Passover holiday in mid-April were booked solid on both El Al and South African Airways.

Even in early 1987, amid all the talk about sanctions, South African officials saw room for growth: In January, South African master chef William Gallagher came to Israel to promote "South Africa Food and Culture Week," scheduled for August and sponsored by the South African Tourism Board, El Al, and a leading Israeli hotel group. Jean-

Paul Rebischung, marketing manager for Europe of the South African Southern Sun Hotel chain, was also in Israel in January to help plan "South Africa Week."

Events such as these are barely newsworthy in Israel. They cause no more excitement and controversy than did, for instance, the 1976 declaration of Cape Town and Haifa as twin cities, the latter a city with a Zionist-Socialist reputation.[19] Similar agreements were signed by Simonstown and Akko, as well as by Durban and Eilat. And in November 1984, the West Bank colony of Ariel signed a twin city agreement with Bisho, the capital of Ciskei. The agreement called for cultural, scientific, industrial, and tourist exchanges, whatever these mean with regard to Bisho and Ariel. "President" Lennox Sebe, who came for the ceremony, was exhilarated: The occasion, he said, was "almost too precious to be scarred by words . . . almost too glorious for ordinary men." Perhaps it was the presence of Knesset members that nearly rendered him speechless. The Israeli legislators "spoke in terms of Israeli-Ciskeian brotherhood and a common struggle against a cruel world of double standards."[20] The *Rand Daily Mail* reported that for Sebe the ceremony and the heavy police escorts that the Israeli authorities sent to protect him were unmistakable signs of the dawning of international recognition. This "shows respect for us from the international community. There are none so blind as those who would not see."[21] In November 1983, those not blind might also have seen a reception for Sebe at Ben-Gurion airport that included dances by bare-breasted African women. In Ciskei proper, Sebe's personal safety has been assured with the help of retired Israeli senior officers (*Maariv*, August 1, 1985, and elsewhere.)

The involvement of establishment Israelis in the Bantustans has deepened despite the displeasure of Foreign Ministry officials whose job is to be concerned with Israel's image and diplomatic prospects in Africa and elsewhere. Nechemia Strassler reported in *Haaretz* that in Ciskei "money talks" and former Finance Minister Yoram Aridor, now a member of the Knesset, is a "most popular personality" and nearly "a member of the family." In April 1985 Aridor and other Knesset members were expected to attend the opening ceremony of the Ciskeian Parliament and watch a military parade of units trained by Israeli officers. Eventually, after heavy pressure from Foreign Ministry officials, only three members of the original delegation left. The *Haaretz* article pointed out that it would be unthinkable for any other politician in the world to visit Ciskei or any other Bantustan.[22] (It does seem impossible to imagine a United States senator who is a regular visitor and investor in a South African "homeland.") Among the other Israeli dignitaries who have regularly visited Ciskei are Former Deputy Finance Minister Yehezkel Flomin, Tel Aviv Deputy Mayor David Griffel, and Ruth Dayan, Moshe Dayan's widow.

Turning to academic contacts, some Israeli professors have readily accepted invitations to tour and lecture in South Africa—as guests of the Pretoria government. The all-expense-paid trip would often include the academics' spouses.[23] Dr. Benjamin Beit-Hallahmi of Haifa University added in a private conversation that more Israeli academics are finding South Africa an acceptable destination for their sabbatical, another practice that would be difficult to find in universities elsewhere. The number of Israeli scholars who have chosen to investigate the ties with their country's "second most important ally after the United States" can easily be counted on the fingers of one hand, as can be seen in the bibliography at the end of this book.

In the past two or three years, the question of relations with South Africa did come up for public debate on a few special occasions, such as before the March 1987 announcement of the Israeli government that it would not increase the number of military contracts it already had with Pretoria (see epilogue). But, as noted, in the early to mid-1980s, there were few such special occasions, and among those few was an instructive Knesset debate about sports ties with South Africa that took place on January 30, 1979, in anticipation of the Moscow Olympics. Dovish Knesset member Yossi Sarid maintained that a distinction must be made between cultural and sports ties on the one hand, and diplomatic and other vital ties on the other. Since the former are optional ties of good will, they should not exist between Israel and South Africa, Sarid suggested. That was too much for Likud Knesset member Dov Shilansky, who chided the Israeli "beautiful souls" who favored Israeli suspension of sports ties with South Africa but did not complain about the participation of Nigeria, Uganda, or Iraq in the Olympics. As for apartheid, Shilanski explained, "I am not saying that I am happy or even agree with the manifestation of separation in South Africa [sic]. I am just saying we have our own problems and let us not poke our noses into the affairs of the whole world."

Shilanski wanted to know if Knesset member Sarid would be consistent enough to demand that Israel cut off its trade with South Africa, or that it abandon the projected power plant near Hadera that would use South African coal mined by cheap black labor. (The question remained unanswered.) The Likud legislator fondly recalled the blessing of a South African cabinet Minister, "State of Israel, good luck to you," which he heard when he visited there. In the spirit of reciprocity, Shilanski urged the Knesset: "Let us honor our friend [South Africa] and wish her good luck as she does to us."[24]

A fuller exposition of why critics of the high-profile relationship with South Africa were afflicted with "naivete, stupidity, and hypocrisy" was offered a year later by Dr. Herzl Rosenblum, a signer of the Israeli Declaration of Independence and the editor of *Yediot Aharonot*, Israel's most popular daily. Rosenblum was incensed about the reception extended to Owen Horwood, reviewed previously. As far as he was concerned, Horwood had been met with unmitigated hostility: "If they only could, our brothers the Jews would have knifed him in the back." But the truth is,

This urge to avoid any contact with Pretoria has its origins in a combination of naivete, stupidity and hypocrisy.

It is naive to suppose that the rest of the world is better than South Africa. And it is naive to suppose that South Africa's enemies which have rallied against her have done so for the sake of the "ideal." And it is naive to suppose that what South Africa's enemies say about her is also what they think about her. . . .

And it is stupidity to suppose that the oppressed majority in South Africa is worse off than the oppressed majority in the Communist bloc and the "non-aligned" dictatorships . . .

And more: the hypocrisy. Well, it is hypocritical to benefit from South Africa and do business under the table with her while venomously assailing her in public. And it is hypocrisy to argue that if the "progressive" countries gained control over South Africa they would have granted her black majority more freedom than the current Pretoria government . . . And, it is hypocrisy to favor non-interference in the domestic affairs of any state and to exclude South Africa from this, whose domestic affairs are everybody's business . . .

How is South Africa worse than Iran and Libya? We even recognized Idi Amin's Uganda and became friends with Idi Amin himself until he humiliated us and expelled us. Is South Africa worse than even Idi Amin's Uganda?. . . .

And more: The blacks in South Africa do not want us or our political assistance. Why do we have to immolate ourselves on their altar in order to overthrow a government which does want us?. . . . Can this be called "statemanship?". . . .

Even if we do all that our "progressives" tell us to do and completely disassociate ourselves from South Africa, our haters will still condemn us, for they hate us not because of our relations with South Africa but rather condemn our relations with South Africa because they hate us, and they will never lack an excuse to hate us. And, the world's hatred with South Africa's friendship is better for us than its hatred without South Africa's friendship.[25]

The Israeli government has repeatedly said it opposes apartheid (chapter 8). In most cases it has also scrupulously avoided condemning the *Pretoria government*. Upon closer examination, many of the "anti-apartheid" statements appear to be fairly ambiguous and not all even mention South Africa, for example, "we cannot be anything but critical of a policy which causes humiliation to others . . . etc., etc."[26] Other Israeli statements did not require any reading between the lines to notice a degree of understanding and empathy for South African whites even as apartheid was termed unacceptable. Thus former Israeli Ambassador I. Unna was asked by the editors of the *Jewish Press* (New York) whether Jewish communities in the United States and elsewhere ought to look favorably upon South Africa because of the "special relationship" between Pretoria and Jerusalem. The interview took place in South Africa and was published the week the Soweto shootings began. Without mentioning apartheid at any point, Unna replied:

I would take my guide line from what the Minister of Tourism Mr. Marais Steyn said to you last night. South Africa is not a Utopia, in fact very few countries are, even Israel is not a Utopia; we all have our shortcomings. Nobody doubts, including the South Africans, that South Africa has its shortcomings, but I do believe that such a visit as yours here, as the guests of the South African Tourist Organization and Pan Am, will enable you to have an honest look at South Africa. You will be able to, I think, divorce hostile propaganda from the reality of the situation, which, I believe, is far more sanguine than the propaganda, the anti-South African propaganda slant tends to make out.[27]

In another instance, an address on the "impressive relationship" between Israel and South Africa, the ambassador went beyond portraying apartheid as a "shortcoming" and "not a Utopia," but even as he did so he described South Africa in terms that are not likely to cross the minds of many other foreign diplomats:

Now it must be clear that, in spite of the good relationship which exists between South Africa and Israel, there can be for us no acceptance of your domestic structure. . . . If we do not join the symphony of nations who constantly breathe down South Africa's neck, it is not because we are not critical of the domestic structure of South Africa, but because we are people who are surrounded ourselves by hordes of counselors. . . . If our voice is not as shrill and as persistent as some would like it to be in the chorus of criticism of South Africa, it is because we have faith in the sincerity of South Africa to tackle these problems and to seek and establish a society which will move away from social injustices. . . .

I would like to say in conclusion that there is one thing I believe South Africa and Israel really share in common and that is a desire to establish a society based on the vision of the prophet Isaiah, a vision of universal peace and the vision of prophets Amos and Micha, the visions of universal justice.[28]

By the summer of 1985, the heavy-handed state of emergency in South Africa was claiming numerous casualties, including children. Pretoria's other allies in the West issued sharp official condemnations as soon as the emergency was declared and then withdrew their ambassadors. The movement towards disinvestment from apartheid was gaining momentum; France banned new investments there.

At a time when the white minority government was isolated as never before, the ties with Israel remained immune to pressures for change. Israel did not issue an official condemnation of the state of emergency and did not recall the ambassador or even offer him a "summer vacation." In mid-August only he and six other ambassadors were still in South Africa, among them those from Chile, Paraguay, and Taiwan.[29] *Haaretz* reported that Foreign Ministry officials were beginning to fear that the Israeli ambassador would find himself alone in Pretoria. But since his term was about to end in the fall, it was decided to wait and see and perhaps delay the departure of his replacement, if that could not be avoided. But by then some Western ambassadors had begun to return and David Ariel, the new Israeli ambassador, was able to leave within days after his predecessor completed his term.

Meanwhile, the *Jerusalem Post* reported that several dozen Israelis demonstrated in Tel Aviv against the state of emergency, some pointing out that the South African security forces were maiming and kill-ing with weapons supplied by Israel. At a cabinet session, Minister of Communications Amnon Rubinstein raised the issue of ties with South Africa. Prime Minister Shimon Peres announced, as reported in *Haaretz*, that "the state of the Jews [sic] will not agree with any discrimination on grounds of race, religion and color."[30] Most ministers had no comment, but Igal Horowitz thought Israel "should not rush" to criticize one of its few friends. No other steps were considered.

Also in August 1985, Chief Buthelezi of the KwaZulu homeland came to Israel on a ten-day visit as a guest of the government. Buthelezi, the only prominent black leader who has campaigned against divestment, is an opponent of the African National Congress (ANC) and the United Democratic Front. It does not seem farfetched to count him as a potential Western-supported "contra" fighting a future radical regime in South Africa. Peres accompanied the visitor to his car, a gesture normally reserved for heads of states. Buthelezi also met with Foreign Minister Shamir and was the guest of honor at a luncheon given by Abba Eban, chairman of the Foreign Affairs Committee of the Knesset. Israeli commentators hailed the visit because it helped maintain contacts with "moderate" [that is, non-ANC] black leaders.

Similarly, in the spring of 1986, the Histadrut labor union provided economic leadership training and taught organizing skills to a delegation of black South Africans. The idea apparently originated with supporters of Israel in the United States, and the South African government made no attempt to stop the delegation. "Some people may want to interpret it as more than it is, but it is just a trade union seminar, nothing more," a spokesman for the Israeli government pointed out, underscoring that the government was not directly involved.[31]

These might have seemed faint, belated attempts to pay some attention to the writing on the wall, amid warnings such as the following by one *Haaretz* columnist: "The day is near when Israel will find that it was a mistake to cling to the bed of the moribund white man to the last moment, at a time when everybody is fleeing from him like from the plague."[32]

But no, the following month Foreign Minister Shamir told the Conference of Presidents of Major American Jewish Organizations that no matter what other governments might do, "We are not going to change the character of our relations with South Africa."[33]

NOTES

1. *New York Times*, July 22, 1985.

2. Yaakov Shimoni in "Israel, the Arabs and Africa," *Africa Report*, July–August 1976.

3. *Die Burger* in 1952, quoted by Gideon Shimoni in *Jews and Zionism: The South African Experience 1910–1967* (Cape Town: Oxford University Press, 1980), p. 221.

4. Zdenek Cervenka and Barbara Rogers, *The Nuclear Axis: Secret Collaboration Between West Germany and South Africa* (New York: Times Books, 1978), p. 311.

5. *Sunday Times* (South Africa) August 11, 1981.

6. Flora Lewis, "Pretoria's Israel Mask," *New York Times*, January 28, 1983.

7. James Markham, "Europeans Give Botha a Frosty Reception," *New York Times*, June 10, 1984.

8. Amnon Abramowitz in *Maariv*, November 9, 1984.

9. Amnon Rubinstein in *Haaretz*, December 12, 1980.

10. *Beeld*, December 10, 1980, in *Jewish Affairs*, January 1981.

11. Amnon Rubinstein in *Haaretz*, December 12, 1980.

12. *Rand Daily Mail*, September 5, 1981.

13. Benjamin Beit-Hallahmi, "South Africa and Israel's Strategy of Survival," *New Outlook: Middle East Monthly* 20:54 April–May 1977, pp. 56–57.

14. *Jerusalem Post*, November 12, 1985.

15. *Oogenblad*, July 30, 1977, in *Jewish Affairs*, September 1977.

16. *Financial Mail* (South Africa) September 14, 1979, p. 18.

17. Rosalynde Ainslee, "Israel and South Africa: An Unlikely Alliance?" United Nations Department of Political and Security Affairs, 1981, # 81-18876, p. 25.

18. *Die Transvaler*, July 27, 1983, in *Jewish Affairs*, September 1983.

19. F. R. Metrowich, *South Africa's New Frontiers* (Sandton: Valiant, 1977), p. 137.

20. Roy Isacowitz, "Twinning with a Tyrant," *Jerusalem Post Magazine*, November 9, 1984.

21. *Rand Daily Mail*, November 15, 1984, in *Jewish Affairs*, January 1985.

22. Nechemia Strassler, "Aridor's Blacks," *Haaretz*, April 11, 1985; *Maariv* weekly overseas edition, April 11, 1985, p. 6.

23. Naomi Chazan, "The Fallacies of Pragmatism: Israeli Foreign Policy Towards South Africa," *African Affairs*, April 1983, p. 183.

24. *Divrei Haknesset* (The Knesset Record), No. 2, January 30, 1979.

25. Herzl Rosenblum, "Al Tmimut, Tipshut Utzviut" ("On Naivete, Stupidity, and Hypocrisy"), *Yediot Aharonot*, January 2, 1981.

26. See for instance a collection of nine Israeli statements, some official, since 1978, in Kenneth Bandler and George Gruen, "Israel and South Africa," A Special Report of the International Relations Department, The American Jewish Committee, New York, 1985, pp. 12–14.

27. *Jewish Press*, June 18, 1976.

28. I. Unna, "Israel and South Africa: An Impressive Relationship," *Zionist Record and South African Jewish Chronicle*, May 20, 1976.

29. *Haaretz*, August 16, 1985, p. 1.

30. *Haaretz*, August 12, 1985, p. 1.

31. *Washington Post*, April 8, 1986.

32. Akiva Eldar in *Haaretz*, August 2, 1985.

33. "Israel Won't Act against Pretoria," *New York Times*, September 27, 1985.

CHAPTER 11

Separatism at the Wrong Time in History?

Israel and South Africa have one thing above all else in common: They are both situated in a predominantly hostile world inhabited by dark peoples.

—*Official Yearbook of the Republic of South Africa*[1]

As the evidence reviewed in the previous chapter suggested, Israel and South Africa do not act at all like reluctant and strange bedfellows. There is a good deal of amity, admiration, and empathy in this relationship. Quite apart from that, the countries have in common much more than interests. One need not dig very far below the surfaces, which are indeed different, to discover that the systems share analogous historical backgrounds, that the logic of their ethnic policies leads in the same direction, or that prevailing political perceptions are similar in both countries. These features, to which we now turn, are distinct enough to set the two countries apart from the rest of today's world; they occupy a unique position in contemporary history.

To be sure, any two political systems can be shown to be similar if the comparison is sufficiently abstract. If, on the other hand, we choose to focus on relatively minor details, the subjects of the comparison will likely seem dissimilar. Are South Africa and Israel similar at a significant level? Do the similarities transcend most internal divisions within each society? The case that they are seems compelling.

Most friends of Israel in the West will, of course, reject such a conclusion a priori. How can anyone compare a democratic society with superior moral standards to a country with institutionalized racism? As a former professor of political science once wrote to the author,

Israel has a working democracy with universal suffrage. . . . South Africa is ruled by a dominant minority. . . . Israel is the historical homeland of the Jewish people and the only homeland it has ever had. The South African whites are people of European stock who left their homeland in search of economic opportunity. . . . Israel has no Bantustans.

Similarly, *Jerusalem Post* columnist Hirsh Goodman was appalled to discover that South African whites find their experiences similar to those of Israel:

When one explains [to Afrikaners] that there is no basis for comparison, one is treated as if one had uttered a blasphemy. One explains that every citizen of Israel is equal in the eyes of the law; that there is freedom of political expression; that there were 31 political parties in the recent Knesset elections from the Marxist left to the right-wing fringe of Meir Kahane. . . .

One points out that Israel is a member of the Socialist International, that it gives equal pay for equal work, that it has the Histadrut labor federation, and does not exploit five out of six citizens for the economic benefit of the minority. One stresses that there is no repressive legislation on Israel's statute book and no discriminatory legislation other than the Law of Return which makes Jews more equal in immigration status than others.[2]

TWO PROMISED LANDS

Before examining the merits of arguments such as those above, it is worth looking at some milestones in the history of Zionism and Afrikanerdom, respectively. This by no means approaches a comprehensive review, nor is it attempted to enter the debate about the merits of various justifications Zionists and South African whites have offered for their acts. If more space is devoted to Israel and Zionism than to South Africa and apartheid, it is because in the West there is far more agreement on the nature of South Africa than on that of Israel.

The movement of political Zionism, as distinct from the spiritual and religious brands of Zionism that existed for centuries, formally began in 1897 with the first Zionist Congress in Basle. In an era of self-determination in Europe, and against a background of anti-Semitism and pogroms, the Zionist movement aimed at settlement and statehood in Palestine. Zionist thinkers such as Herzl and Pinsker concluded that the "Jewish question" had no solution as long as Jews lived among non-Jews: Anti-Semitism goes with being a gentile and is incurable. Only a state where Jews are the majority at all times and the masters of their destiny can correct the tragic course of Jewish history. And where should that special state be established? At first there was no unanimity on that. Until those Zionists who favored Palestine for sentimental and religious reasons prevailed, other options, including Uganda, were briefly considered. At the turn of the century, when political Zionism was born, the overwhelming majority of the residents of Palestine were non-Jewish. Arthur Ruppin, the Zionist historian, wrote that in 1882, Jews numbered some 34,000 out of a population of 300,000.[3]

In 1917 the British cabinet issued the Balfour Declaration, announcing that "His Majesty's government views with favour the establishment in Palestine of a national home for the Jewish people." As far as Zionist leaders were concerned, Palestine was, as one of their better known slogans put it, "a land without a people for a people without a land."[4] Can anything but good come out of developing an "abandoned" and "deserted" land, in dire need of the blessings of Western civilization? The local population, to the extent that the subject came up, would surely benefit from the settlement project, learn modern work methods leading to economic prosperity, and enjoy modern medicine and education. Socialist-Zionist leader Berl Katzenelson, for instance, explained that "never before has the white man undertaken colonisation with that sense of justice and social progress which fills the Jew who comes to Palestine."[5]

But Katzenelson, along with other Zionist leaders such as Chaim Weizmann and David Ben-Gurion, also entertained thoughts of ultimately transferring the non-Jewish majority out of Palestine; their attachment to the land was not too serious and Ben-Gurion found "nothing morally wrong" with the idea of transfer; Yosef Weitz, who became director of the Jewish National Fund in 1932, noted:

It must be clear that there is no room for both peoples in this country. . . . If the Arabs leave the country, it will be broad and wide-open for us. And if the Arabs stay, the country will remain narrow and miserable. . . . and there is no way besides transferring the Arabs from here to the neighboring countries—to transfer them all. Except maybe for Bethlehem, Nazareth and Old

Jerusalem, we must not leave a single village, not a single tribe. And the transfer must be directed to Iraq, to Syria and even to Trans-Jordan.[6]

Berl Katzenelson was in agreement: "The matter of transfer of population raises a dispute among us: permissible or forbidden? My conscience is entirely calm on this matter: better a distant neighbor than a nearby enemy. . . . I believed, and still do, that they must ultimately move to Syria and Iraq."[7]

But unlike the white settlers in southern Africa, the early Zionists did not come to Palestine with economic enrichment in mind. The goals of a self-sufficient Jewish community and eventual statehood required the restructuring of Jewish social life: A Jewish working class and peasantry, strata that did not exist in Europe, had to be created in Palestine. Thus it was not uncommon to see middle-class and professional European Jews who became laborers and peasants in the new land. Yet self-reliance in the midst of a non-Jewish majority had to mean open, deliberate exclusion of Arab labor. For those early Zionists, exclusion was far more important a goal than exploitation; the policy was known as "conquest of labor" or "Hebrew labor." The Histadrut trade union sought quotas for Jewish employment and "civilized" pay rates.[8]

Similarly, in the pre-state period, lands were purchased, typically from absentee landlords, for the purpose of Jewish settlement and farming. The transfer to Jewish ownership was known as "redemption" or "salvaging" of lands (geulat adamot). The resulting dispossession and dislocation of peasants lie at the root of native resistance to Zionism.

In subsequent years the local population did not agree that they were obligated to accomodate Jewish national aspirations in Palestine, a position that they maintained through World War II and the UN partition resolution in 1947. (The latter was seen as a non-binding resolution passed by a Western-dominated body that is not in the business of creating states.) Clearly, what appeared as a reasonable compromise to the settlers was seen in a different light by those who lived on the land where the compromise was to take place, as one might have expected the native population to react anywhere else in the world. They perhaps "wondered why a more appropriate response would not have been to remove the population of Bavaria and turn it into a Jewish state—or . . . why the project could not have been carried out in Massachusetts or New York."[9] During World War II, the United States, Britain, and South Africa were closed to large-scale immigration of Jewish refugees.

The 1948 war, also known in Israel as the "War of Liberation," resulted in a massive exodus of Arabs, three quarters of a million of whom fled or were driven out of Palestine. There was no longer an Arab majority, a relief that first President Chaim Weizmann described as a "miraculous cleaning of the land; the miraculous simplification of Israel's task."[10] The now-simplified task included control of the influx of non-Jews (the Arab refugees were never allowed to return to the Jewish state) while any bona fide Jew in the world was urged to "return." The Israeli government has maintained that the Palestinians should be resettled in Arab states since the Arabs have sufficient funds and states and since they were replaced by Jews from the Middle East.

After independence the government, Zionist institutions, and Jewish settlements set about to gain ownership or control of the great majority of lands within Israel. In his book *Arabs in the Jewish State*, Ian Lustick details some of the methods employed: Much of the land previously owned by those who became refugees in 1948—including those who fled to another area within Israel—was declared "abandoned" and transferred to the Custodian of Absentee Property. The owners were not allowed to reclaim their property even if they were Israeli citizens. As many as half the Arabs in Israel thus became "present absentees" and in many cases saw their lands, houses, and shops taken over by Jewish immigrants. (By 1954 more than a third of the Jewish population lived on "absentee" property.) Other laws, some retroactive, empowered the state to seize lands deemed "uncultivated," "needed for security," or needed for the absorption of Jewish immigration. Inability to prove ownership to the satisfaction of lawyers of the national institutions resulted in the transfer of the "disputed" lands to the state. Another method was to declare an area "closed" under the Emergency Regulations; since the owners were denied access, the land remained uncultivated. "Uncultivated" land could be seized for Zionist projects, another scheme which if perpetrated by an individual might land him in jail.[11]

Until 1966, nearly two decades after the state was established, four out of every five Israeli Arabs lived under "military administration," which permitted detention without trial and restrictions on employment, and barred travel in the country without permits. The large-scale expropriation of lands continued.

Turning to southern Africa, the first permanent European settlement was established in Cape Town in 1652, in an era of outward European expansion. As the settlers moved toward the interior of what is today South Africa, they had to overcome the resistance of the local population, which had been there since the beginning of recorded history. The Khoi-San were the first casualties: Some were driven further north, others died in combat, and still others were assimilated into the racial group known today as "Coloureds." [12] By the 1770s, the forefathers of today's Afrikaners reached far enough north to clash with the Bantu-speaking people, whose colonization, subjugation, and exploitation make up a substantial part of South African history. Today, five million whites are in control of a country in which the Africans number more than 25 million.

Like the Zionists in Palestine, the Boers had to fight not only the local population but the British empire as well. The first "Freedom War" broke out in 1880; the following year the Transvaal was granted autonomy. The second war, which broke out in 1899, was won by the British. At that time the British set up concentration camps for the Boers' families. Many thousands of women and children died, often from starvation or disease. The experience continues to haunt the Afrikaners as a past holocaust of their own. In 1909 the British Parliament passed the South Africa Act that led to the establishment of the Union of South Africa.

While the reasons for settlement and the justifications offered were different, it remains true that in both southern Africa and the Middle East, technologically superior settlers managed to overcome the resistance of a poorly organized local population and establish a political structure in which they have enjoyed superior political, economic, and social status. The armed resistance of the local population is seen in both cases as "terrorism," and hence the most popular organizations among Palestinians and Africans are excluded from negotiations. For their part, in pursuit of security South Africa and Israel have destabilized and repeatedly invaded their neighbors, causing numerous civilian casualties; defied United Nations resolutions; denied civil and political rights; dispossessed and banished opponents. There are no other examples in today's world of embattled Western-oriented outposts facing a hostile Third World population within and without their borders. The last such countries were French Algeria and Rhodesia.

It is axiomatic for both Afrikaners and Zionists that although it was regrettably necessary to fight and win, justice and morality have always been on their side. It is often denied, especially in front of Western audiences, that the local population suffered displacement and tragedy in the process. Among Golda Meir's most familiar statements is the following from a 1969 interview with the *Sunday Times* of London: "It was not as though there was a Palestinian people in Palestine considering itself as a Palestinian people and we came and threw them out and took their country away from them. They did not exist." Hence Israel shares "no, no responsibility whatsoever for their plight." [13] Domestic debates, however, are often more candid: Only weeks before the above interview, Moshe Dayan told a group of students in Haifa:

We came to a land which was populated by Arabs and we are creating a Hebrew state, a Jewish state. In many cases, we purchased the land from Arabs, and the Arab villages were replaced by Jewish villages. You don't even know their names and I do not blame you. Those geography books no longer exist. Not only the books, the villages themselves no longer exist. Nahalal was built in place of Mahaloul, Gevat was built in place of Jivta, Sarid in place of Hanfas. . . . There is not a single settlement which was not built in place of a prior Arab settlement. [14]

Afrikaners have their own brand of revisionist history. As far as many of them are concerned, the early settlers found only primitive "Kaffirs" who came from elsewhere in Africa at about the same time: "The Europeans, including Portuguese, Dutch, British, and Germans have developed South Africa for about 400 years—the early settlers meeting the Black tribes who came down from central Africa to inhabit the lush lands of the north and east of the southern subcontinent." [15]

Under Zionist doctrine, the right to establish a Jewish state in Palestine flows from historical, religious, and even metaphysical reasons. The late Nahum Goldman, a leading dove and former president of the World Zionist Organization observed,

When we appeared on the scene of history, most progressive groups in the world were our best friends. Many of them are no longer. But when these opponents argue that we did the Arabs wrong, that while we may have expelled a large group, hundreds of thousands of people, we have brought it about that they are no longer masters of their land, when one asks "why not give America back to the Indians," the only answer to that is that we have a higher right on our side. . . . We have the higher right for two simple reasons: One is what I would call a metaphysical, a religio-mystical reason, because Jewish history is unthinkable without the central position of Eretz Israel. . . . And the second is the fact that for the Arabs who have large areas of land which they will not have settled in a hundred years, Palestine, which is one or two percent of this area does not play a decisive role.[16]

In the Israeli case, the act of settlement in effect reclaimed an ancient but immutable title to the land, a title that was granted in a divine promise recorded in the *Old Testament*. Not surprisingly, the *Old Testament* claim is seen as compelling even by many Zionists who are otherwise religiously non-observant, such as the late Ben-Gurion. In *Rebirth and Destiny of Israel* he pointed out: "The rights to Palestine do not, as in other countries they do, belong to the existing settlers, whether they be Jews or Arabs. The crux is the Right of Return of Jewry Dispersed."[17]

Similarly, Arieh Eliav, former Secretary General of the Labor Party and today one of Israel's foremost doves, saw fit to point out even as he was calling for a peaceful compromise, "In stating [that the Arabs also have rights] I do not negate or detract one whit from the full historical rights of the Jews to the undivided Land of Israel—that is, the Land of the Twelve Tribes."[18]

The Israeli child in public school begins to study the *Old Testament* as soon as he can read and write. It remains a mandatory subject through graduation from high school. Biblical verse can be heard on the state broadcast media at the beginning and end of each day. Some of the verses mention the conquest of the Land of Canaan and God's desire that the Canaanites be removed or turned into "hewers of wood and drawers of water," their rightful place (Book of Joshua). The attachment to Jerusalem and to the West Bank, which is known in Israeli official statements as Judea and Samaria, the renaming of the currency in recent years as *Shekel* (used by Abraham), and indeed the name *Israel* are additional illustrations of the centrality of the Bible in this twentieth-century state and political movement.

In Afrikaner mythology, one finds a similar role for the Bible as validating their God-given rights. "It was the *Old Testament* and the

doctrine of Calvin that moulded the Boer into the Afrikaner of today,''
Sheila Patterson noted in *The Last Trek*.[19] The Boers were firm believ-
ers that race was destiny: there was that small part of humanity that
was "chosen," and then there was all the rest. The *Old Testament*
read like their own story: An exodus (from the British "Pharaoh")
after which Chosen People are led to a Chosen Land through a miracle
of God; on their way they fight the heathen and suffer from plagues
and droughts. Many of the Boer settlements were given Biblical names:
Betlehem, Nasareth, Bethan, Dalmanutha, and Benoni. It was not difficult to find the right passages in the Bible, for example, Psalm 105:
"He brought forth his people with joy and his chosen with gladness:
and, gave them the lands of the heathen, and they inherited the labour
of the people." The Boers also appreciated the advice given to the
Corinthians in the *New Testament*: "Be ye not unequally yoked together with the unbelievers: for what fellowship hath righteousness
with unrighteousness? Wherefore come out from among them and be
ye separate, saith the Lord, and touch not the unclean thing and I will
receive you."[20]

The Constitution Act, 1961, refers to South Africa as God-given to
a specific people, "this their own" land.[21] Religious programming on
the airwaves is very popular, and some daily newspapers carry scriptural messages. Even "the defence and police forces regard religious
instruction as an indispensable adjunct to the training of recruits," we
are informed in the *Official Yearbook of the Republic of South Africa*,
1982. In short, Afrikaners and their ostracized Dutch Reform Church
have found a way to reconcile apartheid and Christianity. But as a
National Party member of Parliament warned in 1948, "we must be-
ware that our attitude towards the non-European is not so Christian
that it becomes un-Christian towards ourselves and our children."[22]

THE POLICIES OF "CONTRIVED ETHNIC PREPONDERANCE"

There is no a priori reason why in any one state men of different races and
creeds should not be ardent citizens living in peace and harmony with each
other. The trend of modern thought, in spite of backwaters and counter cur-
rents, is surely in that direction. A Russia which must be purely Slav and of
the Orthodox Greek church strikes us as an anachronistic effort.[23]

We now turn to consider the ways in which South Africa and Israel preserve their ''white'' and Jewish characters, respectively. Both efforts can reasonably be viewed as examples of the type of anachronism C. G. Montefiore was referring to in the above passage, which he wrote at the turn of the century.

In South Africa, although biological features have been the determinants of power and privilege for centuries, it was not until 1948, when the National Party took office, that apartheid became official and systematic policy. The Population Registration Act, 1950, is widely seen as the linchpin of apartheid: It classified South Africans as either white, black, Asian, or ''Coloured,'' and the latter category was subdivided further. The act, as amended in 1962, defined a white person as someone who

(a) in appearance obviously is a white person and who is not generally accepted as a Coloured person; or (b) is generally accepted as a white person and is not in appearance obviously not a white person but does not include any person who for the purposes of his classification under this Act, freely and voluntarily admits that he is by descent a native or a Coloured person unless it is proved that the admission is not based on fact.[24]

Classification is subject to change. The Group Areas Act, also passed in 1950, designated the areas where each race may live.[25] Until 1985 when they were abolished, the Pass Laws blocked freedom of movement for Africans, who could legally live only in homelands or townships. Every African over the age of sixteen—and only Africans—required a pass in order to enter the whites' city. Failure to produce the pass at the demand of a police officer was a criminal offense. The Immorality Act (1927, and as amended in 1950 and 1957) and the Prohibition of Mixed Marriages Act (1949), also abolished or prohibited marriage or sex between Europeans and non-Europeans. The legislation allowed police to enter bedrooms to gather evidence. (Even now, however, should an African marry a white woman—in itself never the focus of black struggle in South Africa—it remains unclear where they can legally live and where their children can attend school. Housing and education remain segregated.)

The Reservation of Separate Amenities Act (1953) and the Liquor Act (1977), in conjunction with the Group Areas Act are the bases for what has come to be known as ''petty apartheid.'' This legislation determines which parks, buses, rest rooms, and other facilities are the whites' exclusive domain. Under earlier laws, such as the Native Land Act of 1913 and the Native Trust and Land Act of 1936, the African majority of nearly 74 percent is limited to owning less than one seventh of South Africa's area, land that is mostly eroded although potentially fertile. Today, each of the ethnic groups that comprise the African majority is assigned to a "homeland" or Bantustan, the only places where they may exercise political rights under the "grand apartheid" scheme. Four of the Bantustans are now nominally independent. In November 1983 P. W. Botha received overwhelming white approval for the "new constitution," which provided for a tricameral parliament for whites, Coloureds, and Indians, but excluded the African majority. No other country in the world practices such official and comprehensive discrimination on the basis of biological factors.

In recent years South African leaders have professed to oppose discrimination and apartheid, an "outmoded system," in favor of "power sharing." At the same time, they do not leave the slightest doubt that majority rule is unthinkable and that the cities, classrooms, and entire way of life must remain racially segregated. This brand of white supremacy seems to be driven less by feelings of racial superiority, as was the case in the Verwoerd era, than by the refusal to yield power and privilege.

Would the apartheid legislation have been enacted if the population ratio in South Africa were the reverse of what it is today? Would a white majority, which would result from a hypothetical flight and banishment of most Africans to their "homelands," still need or want their statute books to be explicitly racist? We will never know, but it seems logical that the numerical odds against which supremacy is to be maintained are a major factor.

Israel, by contrast, found its task "miraculuosly simplified," as Chaim Weizmann pointed out. Only about 17 percent of the population is non-Jewish, excluding about 1.2 million Arabs in the territories occupied in 1967. The latter, unlike the Jewish settlers in their midst, are denied political and civil rights. Workers from the West Bank and Gaza commute to Israel daily as inexpensive guest workers. They typically fill construction and janitorial openings and may not stay overnight in pre-1967 Israel. Emergency regulations left over from the British mandate period, comparable to those in effect in South Africa at this writing, are enforced against "terrorists" and their families. Among the measures employed by the authorities have been deportations of leaders and intellectuals without trials, severe censorship and bombing of houses as collective punishment. A new generation of Israelis and Palestinians have grown up under the dual system of politics and law, and all Israeli governments have opposed total withdrawal. The 1967 boundaries have been erased in every sense, including from official Israeli maps.

Naturally, the above features of life under occupation have invited comparisons with South Africa and the Bantustans, but Israeli spokesmen can counter that Israel has not formally annexed the West Bank and is still searching for "authentic" Palestinians (Shimon Peres's term) to negotiate with. In fact, one need not go to the West Bank and Gaza in order to study Israel and Zionism. There is plenty to be learned from pre-1967 Israel. As stated before, since apartheid is more familiar and generates less controversy, it requires less elaboration than Israeli policies.

In the Israeli Declaration of Independence, we find an internal contradiction that seems highly suggestive. It states that "by virtue of our natural and historic right and on the strength of the resolution of the United Nations General Assembly, [we] hereby declare the establishment of a Jewish state in Eretz Israel." The Jewish settlers, having brought "the blessings of progress to all the country's inhabitants" now have a state which "will be open for Jewish immigration and for the Ingathering of the Exiles." But then, in the same paragraph it is stated that the *Jewish* state will "ensure social and political rights to all its inhabitants *irrespective of religion, race or sex.*"[26] A state established by Jews for Jews promised equality to those who were not Jewish. The equality would be as individuals: national rights are a different matter.

Other than the Law of Return (1950) and the Nationality Law (1952), Israeli laws do not distinguish between Jews and non-Jews. The former allows virtually any person in the world whose mother is Jewish or who properly converted to Judaism to become an Israeli citizen upon arrival. The Nationality Law is in fact two laws, one for Jews and the other for non-Jews.[27]

But to say that other Israeli laws are nondiscriminatory is not to say that in the Jewish state government policy is "nationality blind"; and it is not to say that no other mechanism was found to channel vastly superior benefits to Jewish citizens while "lawfully" excluding non-

Jews. The latter is accomplished by "national institutions"—organizations that have been granted quasi-governmental status and have received government funding: the World Zionist Organization, the Jewish Agency, and The Jewish National Fund. These Zionist organizations promote Jewish immigration, Jewish settlement, and Jewish land acquisition. The Jewish Agency, for instance, has played a key role in developing the infrastructure and housing in Jewish areas. If new Jewish settlements have roads and electricity while older and larger Arab villages don't, no one can point to a discriminatory Israeli law or cabinet resolution that is directly responsible. As Ian Lustick explains:

Because they are not formally part of the Israeli government apparatus, they do not serve a constituency of Israeli citizens. . . . They therefore constitute efficient conduits for channeling resources to the *Jewish* population only, resources which are converted into capital-intensive economic development projects, educational vocational training, social services, land acquisition, etc. In the implementation of such programs, officials of these institutions see themselves ideologically as well as legally justified in ignoring the needs of Arab Israelis and the impact of their activities on the Arab sector.[28]

Not only is there no appearance of "separate development" formally originating from the government, the government may point out, as it does regularly, that Israeli Arabs are materially better off than those in surrounding countries.

Still, government spending in the Arab sector is far lower than in the Jewish sector. All in all, the gap between Arab and Jewish settlements is striking, whether one compares housing, employment opportunities, health services, education, or numerous other indicators. This is how the two Nazareths, one Jewish and the other Arab, both within pre-1967 Israel, compared in the 1970s:

Upper Nazareth, which was built some 15 years ago "in order to create a counterweight to Arab Nazareth" constitutes a cornerstone of the "Judaization of the Galilee" policy. Upper Nazareth was erected upon the hills surrounding Nazareth as a security belt surrounding it almost on all sides. It was built upon thousands of acres of land which were expropriated high-handedly, purely and simply by force, from the Arab settlements, particularly Nazareth and Rana. . . . The visitor to Nazareth can notice with his own eyes the neglect and lack of development of the city, and if he then goes "up" to Upper Nazareth he will see the new buildings, the wide streets, the public lights, the steps, the tall buildings, the industrial and artisan enterprises and he will be able to notice the contrast: development up there and neglect down there, constant government construction up there and none whatsoever down there. Since 1966, the Israeli Ministry of Housing has not built a single apartment in old Nazareth.[29]

Although no state law explicitly denies access to Israeli Arabs, "public" lands—also known as "state" lands—have been effectively reserved for Jewish use with legal mechanisms such as the Jewish National Fund (JNF), the Custodian of Absentee Property, the Land Administration, and the Jewish Agency Settlement Department. Non-Jewish citizens of Israel have been excluded from long-term leasing or development of approximately 92 percent of the lands in the pre-1967 borders.[30] The Jewish National Fund charter mandates that lands controlled by the Fund must remain the property of the Jewish people indefinitely and cannot be sold, leased, or rented to non-Jews. Nor can non-Jewish labor be employed on such "public" lands. In the fall of 1985, a JNF official confirmed that the rules are still in effect; an extensive report on these and other Israeli practices in the September 27 *Haaretz* supplement found that the parallels with South Africa are remarkable.

Technically, what the JNF charter calls for is not legally binding on the state, but one could hardly tell this from the experiences of Palestinians in Israel.

The Ministry of Agriculture and the Settlement Department of the Jewish Agency have recently launched a vigorous campaign to eradicate the plague of leasing land and orchards to Bedouins and Arab farmers in the western Galilee.

The director of the Galilee Area for the Jewish Agency, Mr. Aharon Nahumi, said that his office had sent a memorandum to all settlements in which they are warned that the leasing of national lands to be cultivated by Arab share-croppers, as well as renting the orchards for the purpose of picking and marketing by Arabs, is against the law and the regulations of the Settlement Authorities and settlement movements.

The management of the Galilee area is calling on the settlements to refrain from this conduct and is underscoring that last year the Department pressed charges against those settlements which did not comply.[31]

The differential effects of military service on Jews and Arabs in Israel are also highly significant. The overwhelming majority of Israeli

Arabs do not have to, nor can they volunteer, to serve in the armed forces. But being a veteran is often among the requirements listed in descriptions of job openings, even when the position has not a thing to do with security. Similarly, many benefits (for example, government-backed mortgages, welfare payments aimed at encouraging large families, and scholarships) have been conveniently made contingent on past military service of the recipient—or someone in the family. Thus welfare benefits for those whose "parents, grandparents, or brothers served in the IDF" were set 40 percent higher; but that would still have inadvertently discriminated against Jewish religious seminary students who are exempted from military service. A solution had to be found, and was, in the form of a special fund for such students under the control of the Ministry of Religion.[32]

A similar pattern of discrimination practiced behind a thin fig leaf can be found in the network of state-run employment agencies that guarantee that Jewish workers have the first claim on job openings. Most Jews live in or near industrialized areas or high-incentive "development zones"; Arab areas are neither industrialized, nor do they qualify as "development zones." Predictably, the employment agencies are required to give preference to workers from the immediate area. In times of unemployment, we would expect Arab areas to be hit hardest. When there is full employment, the system ensures that the better jobs go to Jewish workers with Arabs being able to fill only whatever may be left.

Since all the above forms of discrimination are "lawful," they cannot be challenged in any Israeli court. Furthermore, the courts are likely to reject appeals "without further need of specification or substantiation" whenever the state claims that this or that action was undertaken for security considerations.[33]

Given the character of the state, it is unavoidable that a major preoccupation would be the difference between Arab and Jewish birth rates, the key ingredient in the "demographic nightmare." Israeli planners have given the issue much thought. One milestone was a confidential memorandum, "Handling the Arabs of Israel," written for Prime Minister Izhak Rabin in 1976 and leaked to *Al Hamishmar*. Written by Israel Koenig, Northern District Commissioner of the Ministry of the Interior, the document proposed ways to overcome the imbalance between the 5.9 percent annual rate of increase in the Arab population versus only 1.5 percent for Jews. Koenig observed that in the past the state had failed to take into account "the Arab character which is Levantine and superficial, which contains no depth, and in which the activity of the imagination is greater than that of the reason." It was necessary, he wrote, to get serious about the problem and adopt such measures as "expand and deepen Jewish settlement in areas where the contiguity of the Arab population is prominent and where they number considerably more than the Jewish population; examine the possibility of diluting existing Arab population concentrations." It would also help to reduce the number of Arab students in Israeli universities, make it easy for them to study abroad but difficult to return, cut allowances to large Arab families, and institute employment quotas. The greater economic hardship should deny them the "social and economic security that . . . grants them, consciously and subconsciously, leisure for 'social-nationalist' thought."[34] Ian Lustick believes that "the document as a whole reflects more clearly and comprehensively than any other published source the overall orientation toward the Arab minority of those officials with responsibility for the affairs of the non-Jewish population.[35] Naturally, after the memorandum became public, Koenig neither offered his resignation nor was asked to do so by his superiors.

As the territories, but not the residents, of West Bank and Gaza became increasingly integrated within Greater Israel, solutions to the "demographic nightmare" that involve deportation or denial of elementary rights came out of the closet in Israeli politics. Deputy speaker of the Knesset Meir Cohen believes that "Israel made a grave mistake [in 1967] by not expelling 200,000 to 300,000 Arabs from the West Bank."[36] In late 1984 the Public Opinion Research Institute (PORI) found that just under 30 percent of Israeli Jews accepted some or all of Knesset Member Meir Kahane's positions on Palestinians.[37] Kahane, one of whose slogans is "I say what you think" and who often begins his speeches with the greeting "Hello Jews, hello dogs" was gaining considerable legitimacy and popularity in 1984–1985. Thomas Friedman observed in a front page *New York Times* report, "Today no one is dismissing Rabbi Kahane," whose appeal extends even to segments of "centrist Israeli society." These are the Israelis who wish to "end what they call the 'Arab problem' once and for all."[38] In an update the following year (November 13, 1986), Friedman reported that for various reasons Meir Kahane the person had lost popularity even as the ideology of Kahanism was gaining ground in Israel.

Already in 1984, 15 percent of the Israeli public favored the deportation of Palestinian residents of the occupied territories to Arab states; about as many were willing to grant them full civil rights in Israel, while a substantial plurality (43.5 percent) had no objection to the Palestinians' presence—without voting and other political rights.[39] At least in this poll, conducted by Dr. Mina Zemach for the respected Dahaf Institute, a majority of the Israeli public chose deportation or apartheid.

Thirty-six percent of the Israeli Jewish public regards Arabs as "dirty," according to another poll by Zemach reported on the front page of *Maariv*, which she describes as scientific and representative.

Forty-two percent consider Arabs "primitive," 33 percent think of them as "not valuing human life," and 41 percent as "violent." Thirty-six percent of the respondents opposed equal rights for Arabs and Jews, two in every three opposed the sale of lands to Arabs in the central region of the country, and one in three believed that a way should be actively sought to bring about Arab emigration.[40] Israeli officials are also on record as having referred to the presence of Arabs or their labor as a "cancer."[41] A few reports in the Israeli press told of prison terms for Arabs who pretended to be Jews. (No Jews are known to have pretended to be Arabs.) Thus we read that one Arab was "suspected of having posed as a Jew and promised to marry a widow" with whom, it was further "suspected," he had had an intimate relationship. The offending Arab was detained by the Fraud Squad of Haifa police.[42] (In Israel, there is no legal provision for Jewish-Arab marriages. All marriages performed there must be religious, and in the case of Jews only those performed by Orthodox rabbis are valid.)

In July of 1985, the local council of Kiryat Arba, the Jewish settlement near Hebron, passed a resolution to "take immediate action to terminate the employment of all Arabs employed by the local council and to arrange for street maintenance and gardening to be performed by contractors who will only employ Jews . . . to award permits and recommendations only to businesses or investors whose line of business and declarations guarantee that only Jews will be employed and who will not establish joint enterprises with Arabs."[43]

Is Zionism, then, a form of racism as the UN General Assembly stated in 1975? The question stands little chance of being settled in this chapter. Yet in a land with growing numbers of non-Jews, policies of "separate development" in some form or another are inevitable if

Zionist ideology is to be implemented. Such policies need not be, and at present cannot be, found in the letter of most Israeli laws. The more complex and less visible mechanisms have managed to "serve the ideological ends of Zionism while reaping propaganda benefits among liberal circles abroad," Lustick observed. But just as it would be reasonable to expect in the case of a state established to serve the interests of all Moslems or Christians or blacks in the world, Israel cannot and does not belong to all its citizens. With national goals such as "ingathering of exiles," being "the sovereign state of all Jewish people," and maintaining a Jewish majority, the avowed character of the state is a significant departure from contemporary Western notions of secular citizenship rights and political pluralism. And it is at best misleading to describe Israel as "Jewish" in the same sense that France is French: The latter does not officially strive to be the country of one ethnic group or race. Arabs living in the French state are French, but Arabs living in the Jewish state are not Jewish.

It is worth noting that the above ethnic and religious exclusivism can override differences in skin color, as the acceptance of Ethiopian Jews demonstrates. Predictably, the main problem they presented was whether they were genuine Jews, that is, biologically descended from an ancient Jewish tribe. Most rabbis ultimately ruled they were, though in order to be on the safe side the immigrants were requested to "renew" their Jewishness by immersing themselves in the *mikvah* ritual baths and to obtain a document certifying their status as Jews. Black Hebrews from the United States, by contrast, were found by an Israeli court in 1972 not to be genuine Jews. The authorities began to deport them in 1984. Since then there have been numerous reports of black American tourists who were suspected of being black Hebrews and questioned at length, had their passports confiscated to guarantee that they do not stay too long in the Jewish state or were required to post bonds worth thousands of dollars.

South African whites, who did not enjoy the luxury of becoming a majority due to mass flight or deportation of the indigenous population to the "homelands," had to adopt more overt measures in order to maintain supremacy. The black masses were seen as inferior objects of exploitation and, in the same breath, as a formidable threat to survival.[44] The European colonizers made a distinction between the "civilized" (Christian) part of the human race and the (heathen) savages. And the Africans, as George Frederickson noted, appeared to these colonizers to be closer to beasts than to humans. It was an urgent task to try to rescue those savages from ignorance and darkness.[45]

While such attitudes are (arguably) no longer driving the engine of apartheid, bigotry and prejudice remain pervasive. In a 1985 book on South African whites, the author, Vincent Crapanzano, was repeatedly told about black inferiority, laziness, and stupidity. One farmer who lives north of Cape Town explained that "the Black man thinks slowly" and then noted: "The relationship between whites and Coloureds is very good. . . . The farmers treat them well. No farmer would treat his horse badly because he has to use it. It would be foolish. It is the same with the workers."[46]

At the root of apartheid is the definition of nationality in monoracial and unicultural terms. For the purpose of preserving a "white" South Africa, apartheid has designated special homogeneous homelands for each group, a practice also known as "macro-segregation." As noted, other legislation regulates smaller scale segregation at the local level, for example, the Group Areas Act, the Bantu Education Act, and the now-abolished Prohibition of Mixed Marriages Act.

No Israeli equivalent can be found for the latter type of official segregation, or "micro-segregation." Yet the anti-pluralist, exclusivist tendencies of Zionism do converge with the central tenet of macro-segregation: *The concept of one-person one-vote in a pluralistic state shared by the settlers and the indigenous population that these settlers found is as unthinkable under Zionism as it is under apartheid.* In both cases the original population is treated as if they were aliens, while those who came from elsewhere and their immediate descendants have assumed the role of natives. In Israel, for instance, a Jewish American is granted upon arrival rights vastly superior to those of any Israeli citizen who is an Arab and whose family has lived there for generations. The notion that the native population should enjoy the same status and rights as the settlers is beyond the bounds of "civilized" discussion in Israel, in fact even more so than in South Africa.

If similar anachronistic concepts of citizenship were applied to the United States, it would be juridically and demographically an Anglo-Saxon, Christian America, just as in the above example the Soviet Union would be a purely Slav Russia. Such approaches parallel tribal *kinship* concepts as well as German nationalistic *Volk* thought.[47]

South Africa and Israel do go beyond most modern democratic polities in their anti-pluralistic character. Thus while it is not uncommon for modern democratic nations to be open to some outsiders and closed to others, the legal criteria for admission and benefits are not normally racial, religious, or cultural. Yet Jewish Israel and white South Africa can only be what they are now: Secular citizenship rights cannot be granted because that would mean the end of the polity as currently constituted. The world was more hospitable to such political systems a century or two or three ago; towards the end of the twentieth century and in this post-colonial era, Zionism and apartheid do encounter their share of public relations problems. It is the struggle to preserve this type of *Herrenvolk* democracy at what is evidently an inauspicious time in history that, above all else, makes South Africa and Israel natural bedfellows.

The dream of apartheid calls for a white South Africa with autonomous black Bantustans; the implementation of Zionism calls for a predominantly Jewish Israel with safeguards against a radical change in the demographic balance. The Likud Party favors annexation and, as a solution for the Palestinian "problem," autonomy under "moderate leadership" within Greater Israel (with more limitations than the South African Bantustans—internal security, Jewish settlements, water rights, "state" lands, etc.) The Labor Party prefers "territorial compromise" for areas densely populated with Arabs; it may accept a Palestinian-Jordanian "homeland" of sorts, provided it is not a sovereign state.

Heribert Adam explained why polities such as Israel and South Africa must be seen as fundamentally different from the many other states where discrimination can be found:

In most hierarchically organized systems certain ethnic segments have a politically inferior status. They are not merely excluded from the spoils of political power as in many divided peripheries but the state itself is defined in terms of the myths and symbols of the ruling group as its exclusive domain. In these ethnic states the ruling group ideology is enshrined in law or custom at the expense of secular citizenship rights. There are second-class citizens, almost outside the polity who are perceived as untrustworthy by birth.[48]

There is nothing in what was said so far that would rule out a considerable degree of freedom for members of the dominant segment of the population in each country, especially if dissent remains within the parameters of state ideology. One finds that both countries hold free elections and grant freedom of speech and freedom of the press, often to a greater extent than in surrounding Third World states. (In Israel, however, the nonobservant must constantly face the consequences of the lack of separation between church and state.) Still, restricted to the above criteria, Israel and South Africa are "two of the only 30 democracies in the world," as Israeli Minister of Industry and Commerce Gideon Pat pointed out in earnest in Pretoria.[49]

THE SEA OF HOSTILITY

There are telling similarities in the ways dominant groups in South Africa and Israel view the world. From the perspective of a fortress mentality, the world is unjustly hostile, a "pack of wolves" ganging up with double standards and not the slightest regard for fairness, truth, or principles. The hostility is just there, and always for reasons other than what the regimes do at home or abroad.[50] The majority of Third World nations is seen as at best indifferent to whether terrorists and their backers manage to destroy the settler state (or, more crudely put, "throw them into the sea.") Only their own power can insure their survival. What others think makes no difference: "It does not matter what the gentiles say, only what the Jews do," Prime Minister David Ben-Gurion used to say, which is still one of the most popular political slogans in Israel. No one in the world has the right to "teach them morality" or tell them which measures are necessary for their security.

If the world is critical, it can only be, as President Chaim Herzog wrote in his book *Who Stands Accused?*, because of the Third World "automatic majority" and the West, which is "succumbing to the power of oil and commercial interests." And further, "We repesent principles and values which are so distasteful to many regimes in the world that we must continue to expect the outpouring of calumnies against the Jewish people and Israel to which we must become accustomed."[51]

If the last four years at the United Nations prove anything, it is that our enemies do not distinguish in any way between Israel and the Jewish people. . . . These resolutions, which were drafted by the P.L.O. and the Arab states, recall from the shadows of the past the racist interpretations of Der Stürmer in Nazi Germany. The violent anti-Semitic tone which has been injected into these resolutions is gradually joining the automatic slogans of vilification and hate which have become part of the international political vocabulary in the Soviet and so-called non-aligned world.[52]

White South Africans also find that the world has refused to understand them and to this day continues to humiliate, besmirch, and unjustly pressure them. As early as 1946, the infant United Nations was described by Jan Christian Smuts as afflicted with a "solid mass of prejudice against the colour policies of South Africa," prejudices which cannot be neutralized by even the "most efficient publicity."[53] Daniel Malan saw a world that temporarily lost its senses about South Africa due to a "sickly sentimentality with regard to the Black man"; Verwoerd spoke of "psychosis" in the West about freedoms of blacks in South Africa; P. W. Botha saw a "paralysis in the mind of the West" that keeps it from seeing the importance of South Africa and becoming involved in "the fight for Christian civilised standards." But the essence of evil remains the United Nations, that "hydra-headed animal" conspiring to "contract us out of existence," as Roelof Botha put it.[54]

Those who are politically active against South Africa do so out of maliciousness, vindictiveness, prejudice, ignorance, or anti-white racism. They are, as a matter of fact, bent on destroying the whites. As P. W. Botha stated:

Like the rest of the Free World, the Republic of South Africa (RSA) is a target for international communism and its cohorts—leftist activists, exaggerated humanism, permisiveness, materialism and related ideologies. In addition, the RSA has been singled out as a special target for the by-product of their ideologies, such as Black racialism, exaggerated individual freedom, one-man one-vote and a host of other slogans employed against us on the basis of double standards.[55]

This is all part of the aforementioned "Total Onslaught," which includes all possible forms of pressure on South Africa: persuasion, coercion, boycotts, and diplomatic isolation. The Onslaught (read calls to end white supremacy) is seen in Manichaean terms as a manifestation of the ongoing struggle between Western civilization and communism, its deadly enemy. Although communist-inspired, the Onslaught includes the United Nations, the Organization of African Unity, and even the West. Since the West wants to force the South African government to abdicate, as did Rhodesia's, they are in fact, according to Defense Minister Magnus Malan," available as the handymen of the communists and they are indirectly contributing to the destruction of capitalism and the establishment of world communism."[56] This, as one scholar noted, is a "permanent invitation for the Western nations to embrace the apartheid regime as their ideological kin and to include it within their collective security system."[57]

The theme of a "communist master plot" to conquer the world, in most cases with South Africa as the first stepping-stone, is indeed omnipresent in South African official statements and writings. The blindness and weakness of the West is regularly contrasted with the rapaciousness of the communists who remain adamant in their desire to rule the world. For instance, the 1367 page report of a judicial commission to the South African parliament, published in 1982, saw the hand of the Soviet Union in the attempts to weaken South Africa with the goal of denying minerals and oil to Western Europe. That would place the cunning communists in a better position to attack the United States. Soviet proxies, such as the African National Congress and the Pan Africanist Congress, are useful tools for this dark purpose. The premise is that there would be no race conflict in South Africa if not for outside agitation.[58] Prime Minister P. W. Botha was once even able to tell an interviewer in what order the communists planned to conquer the world: Europe first, then Africa for its raw materials and Cape Sea route, next they would isolate the United States from Europe, and then proceed to assault China.[59]

Although Israeli official statements do not normally go so far, the assumptions of the cold war are widely shared. The "common ideal" to which Prime Minister Rabin and his guest Prime Minister Vorster drank in Jerusalem (chapter 4) was indeed to resist "foreign-inspired instability and recklessness"; Defense Minister Ariel Sharon saw the need for the West to break the embargo and supply South Africa with additional weapons on grounds that it is one of the few countries in Africa and Southwest Asia trying to resist "Soviet infiltration," which is "gaining ground daily."[60]

As part of its contribution to what it sees as "the defense of the West," Israel has armed and trained numerous armies and police forces of murderous right wing dictatorships, among them Chile, Zaire, Haiti, the Philippines, and Guatemala. (As noted, Israel was also among a handful of United States allies that were invited to join the "Star Wars" project; it was the third country to accept, after Britain and West Germany.)

The collapse of white rule in South Africa would be bad news for Jerusalem not only because of the important relationship or the anti-communist orientation, but also because it is understood that more Third World and United Nations heat may then be turned on Israel. As A. Schweitzer explained in *Haaretz* in the summer of 1985:

The Third World, with Soviet guidance and Arab financing, has for years been on the offensive against two states which are linked with the West: Israel and South Africa. . . . It should be clear to anyone who has eyes in his head that the fall of either of these states will accelerate the assault on the other. We would therefore not be doing ourselves a favor if we rush to mourn South Africa or speed up her decline by diplomatic or other action. On the contrary, we should hope it overcomes the current crisis.[61]

Former Israeli Ambassador in Pretoria I. Unna was also concerned about South Africa, which "must be seen as having special values for the Free World." Should its enemies prevail, he feared, it would be a "frightful situation—one that would make any discussion about racial equality, or even improvements in the racial situation, completely irrelevant. It would be a disaster if South Africa were lost as a constructive and active member of the free community of nations."[62]

NOTES

1. Republic of South Africa, *South Africa Yearbook* (Johannesburg: The Information Service of South Africa, 1977 ed.), p. 61.

2. Hirsh Goodman, "Parallel Illusions," *Jerusalem Post Magazine*, September 11, 1981.

3. Arthur Ruppin, *Jews in the Modern World* (New York: Arno Press, 1973), p. 368.

4. See for instance Amos Elon, *The Israelis: Founders and Sons* (New York: Holt, Rinehart & Winston, 1971), p. 149.

5. Quoted by Stanley Greenberg in *State in Capitalist Development: Comparative Perspectives* (New Haven: Yale University Press, 1980), p. 357.

6. Yosef Weitz in *My Diary and Letters to the Children*, quoted by Edward Said, *The Question of Palestine* (New York: Times Books, 1979), pp. 99–100.

7. Katzenelson's *Writings*, as quoted by author Moshe Shamir, *Maariv*, August 9, 1974.

8. Greenberg, *State in Capitalist Development*, pp. 360–65.

9. Noam Chomsky, *The Fateful Triangle: The United States, Israel and the Palestinians* (Boston: South End Press, 1983), p. 92.

10. Quoted by Ian Lustick, *Arabs in the Jewish State: Israel's Control of a National Minority* (Austin: University of Texas Press, 1980), p. 28. The "miracle" notwithstanding, in 1979 five Israeli cabinet members acting as a censorship board "prohibited former Prime Minister Izhak Rabin from including in his memoirs a first person account of the expulsion of 50,000 Palestinian civilians from their homes near Tel Aviv during the 1948 Arab-Israeli war." David K. Shipler, *New York Times*, October 23, 1979.

Nadav Safran of Harvard University, who is above suspicion of being anti-Israeli, noted in his book *From War to War: The Arab-Israeli Confrontation 1948–1967* (Indianapolis, Ind.: The Bobbs-Merrill Co., 1969) that "on the basis of first hand observation it can be said that until about the end of May–early June 1948 the refugees from areas under Jewish control left, and left in the face of persistent Jewish efforts to persuade them to stay. From that point on they were *expelled* from almost all new territories that came under Israeli control . . . "—about as many as those who left voluntarily. The Zionists "thought it advantageous to have in it a homogeneous population and proceeded to push the Arabs out" (pp. 34–35).

Of those not evicted, many fled in terror after the Dir Yassin massacre carried out by Menachem Begin's Irgun. Referring to the "enemy propaganda" in the aftermath of the massacre, Begin wrote in his book *The Revolt*: "In the result, it helped us. Panic overwhelmed the Arabs of Eretz Israel . . . the Arabs began to flee in terror even before they clashed with Jewish forces." The Arabs of Haifa for instance, "began fleeing in panic, shouting: Dir Yassin!" *The Revolt* (Los Angeles: Nash Publishing, 1972), pp. 164–65.

Israeli spokesmen, on the other hand, have argued that Arab leaders called upon the population to leave temporarily so as to make it easier for the Arab armies to rout the Israelis. The assertion has not been backed up with sufficient evidence. Nor is it obvious that, even if that *were* the major cause of Palestinian flight, those who listened to the above calls automatically forfeited their rights to their homes, lands, and shops.

11. Lustick, *Arabs in the Jewish State*, pp. 51, 57–59, 172–78. So that his motives will not be questioned, the author makes it clear in the preface that "all my life I have been involved, as a participant, leader and resource person, in Jewish and Zionist organizations."

12. For a comprehensive history, see the two-volume *Oxford History of South Africa* by Monica Wilson and Leonard Thompson (New York: Oxford University Press, 1971).

13. *Sunday Times* (London), June 15, 1969.

14. The address was reprinted in *Haaretz*, April 4, 1969.

15. Brigadier Jack Penn, in *Armed Forces* (South Africa) April 1980.

16. Nahum Goldman, "Basle 1897-Israel 1967: Assembly to Mark the 70th Anniversary of the Foundation of the Zionist Congress," pp. 27–28. Quoted in Bhim Singh, *An Examination of Documents on which the State of Israel Is Based* (Beirut: PLO Research Center, 1970).

17. Quoted by Hassan Haddad, "The Biblical Bases of Zionist Colonialism," in Ibrahim Abu-Lughod and Baha Abu Laban, *Settler Regimes in Africa and the Arab World: The Illusion of Endurance* (Wilmette, Ill.: Medina University Press International, 1974), p. 8.

18. Arieh Eliav, "We and the Arabs," *Foreign Policy* #10, Spring 1973, p. 64.

19. Sheila Patterson, *The Last Trek: A Study of the Boer People and the Afrikaner Nation* (London: Routledge & Kegan Paul, 1957), p. 177; See also George Frederickson, *White Supremacy: A Comparative Study in American and South African History* (New York: Oxford University Press, 1981).

20. Quotes in John Fisher's *The Afrikaners* (London: Cassel & Co., 1969), p. 38.

21. Wilson and Thompson, *Oxford History of South Africa*, p. 371.

22. Patterson, *The Last Trek*, p. 207.

23. C. G. Montefiore, as quoted by Ali A. Mazrui, "Zionism and Apartheid: Strange Bedfellows or Natural Allies?" *Alternatives*, no. 9, Summer 1983, p. 77.

24. Wilson and Thompson, *Oxford History of South Africa*, p. 403.

25. For fuller details, see Leo Marquard, *The Peoples and Policies of South Africa* (New York: Oxford University Press, 1969), especially pp. 129–35.

26. Text in *Encyclopaedia Judaica*, (Jerusalem: Keter Publishers, 1972), 5, col. 1453–1454. (Emphasis added.)

27. On occasion, questions arise about the authenticity of a prospective immigrant or his parents' "Jewishness." "Additional documentation" is then required, and the ordeal that often results is fit to print in the daily newspapers. For the story of one such couple, see Shaul Hon, "Playing with the Law of Return," *Maariv*, May 17, 1985.

28. Lustick, *Arabs in the Jewish State*, p. 106.

29. Joseph Elgazi in *Zo Haderech*, July 30, 1975; See also Greenberg, *State in Capitalist Development*, p. 368.

30. Lustick, *Arabs in the Jewish State*, pp. 107–8.

31. *Maariv*, July 3, 1975.

32. Lustick, *Arabs in the Jewish State*, pp. 94, 292.

33. Sammy Smooha and Don Peretz, "The Arabs in Israel," *Journal of Conflict Resolution*, September 1982, p. 477.

34. *Al Hamishmar*, September 7, 1976; Lustick, *Arabs in the Jewish State*, pp. 68–69, 256.

35. Lustick, *Arabs in the Jewish State*, p. 69.

36. *New York Times*, April 4, 1983.

37. *Haaretz*, December 11, 1984. Additional reports on the widespread support for Kahane among the youth can be found in *Maariv* Weekly Magazine, June 28, 1985; Danny Rubinstein, "The Irony of Israel's Democracy Project," *New York Times*, July 16, 1985.

38. *New York Times*, August 5, 1985.

39. *Al Hamishmar*, July 20, 1984.

40. *Maariv*, August 19, 1980. See also Smooha and Peretz, "The Arabs in Israel," especially p. 476.

41. Aaron Uzan, then Minister of Agriculture, told a kibbutz audience that "the domination of Jewish agriculture by Arab workers is a cancer in our body." (*Haaretz*, December 13, 1974); similarly, in 1979, three years after the aforementioned Koenig report, the Northern Israeli Military Commander described the Arabs of the Galilee as a "cancer." See Lawrence Meyer, *Israel Now: Portrait of a Troubled Land* (New York: Delacorte Press, 1982), p. 270; and former Chief of Staff Raphael Eytan explained to a Knesset committee in 1983 that "when we have settled the land, all the Arabs will be able to do about it will be to scurry around like drugged roaches in a bottle." *New York Times*, April 14, 1983.

42. *Maariv* overseas edition, October 16, 1981, p. 7. See also *Yediot Aharonot*, April 20, 1979; *Haaretz*, July 28, 1977.

43. *Maariv*, July 26, 1985.

44. Wilson and Thompson, *Oxford History of South Africa*, II, p. 366.

45. Frederickson, *White Supremacy*, passim.

46. Vincent Crapanzano, *Waiting: The Whites of South Africa* (New York: Random House, 1985), pp. 317–18.

47. Mazrui, "Zionism and Apartheid," p. 75.

48. Heribert Adam, "Ethnic Politics and Crisis Management: Comparing South Africa and Israel," *Journal of Asian and African Studies*, 18, nos. 1–2, 1983.

49. Yoav Karni, "Dr. Shekel and Mr. Apartheid," *Yediot Aharonot*, March 13, 1983.
As for the right of Israeli Arabs to vote, they have had effective access only to Rakah, the "pariah" Communist party; some Arabs have run for the Knesset in "Arab lists" affiliated with the major Zionist parties. These "lists" are not parties, have no steady membership, and their names may vary from one election to the next. They are, however, useful as "vote-catching tactics" for

as long as the candidates refrain from "exhibiting tendencies toward independence in their political stands." See Lustick, *Arabs in the Jewish State*, pp. 208–9.

50. Friends of Israel argue that South Africa is being opposed for its domestic policies, while Israel is being opposed "because it exists." One suspects that if South Africa had a powerful lobby in the West, it would also argue, at a comparable intellectual level, that all the whites want is self-determination in their homeland—as if that did not involve displacement, exclusion, and discrimination.

51. Chaim Herzog, *Who Stands Accused? Israel Answers Its Critics* (New York: Random House, 1978), p. 17.

52. Ibid., pp. 140–41.

53. Deon Geldenhuys, *The Diplomacy of Isolation: South African Foreign Policy Making* (New York: St. Martin's Press, 1984), p. 209.

54. Ibid.

55. Department of Defence of the Republic of South Africa, "White Paper on Defence and Armament Production," 1973.

56. Deon Geldenhuys, *The Diplomacy of Isolation*, p. 209.

57. Edouard Bustin in Onkar Marwah and Ann Schulz, *Nuclear Proliferation and the Near Nuclear Countries* (Cambridge, Mass.: Ballinger Publishing Co., 1975), p. 217.

58. The report was discussed in *New York Times*, February 7, 1982, p. E3.

59. Anna Starcke, *Survival* (Cape Town: Tafelberg Publishers, 1978), p. 57.

60. *New York Times*, December 14, 1981.

61. A. Schweitzer, "Madua Drom Africa" ("Why South Africa?"), *Haaretz*, August 6, 1985.

62. *To the Point*, July 27, 1979, in *Jewish Affairs*, September 1979.

CHAPTER 12

Epilogue: Some Call These Sanctions

Israel and South Africa, this book has contended from the start, are not and do not act like strange bedfellows. Their partnership has rested on a community of interests and complementary resources, but that is far from the entire story. As the world's two remaining political systems committed to separatist philosophies that exclude indigenous Third World majorities, they have developed an underlying sense of kinship and solidarity. This sense can only intensify in the foreseeable future and beyond, as resistance, "iron fist" state violence and counterviolence spread in both areas. It was also noted that neither country would welcome the weakening or political demise of the other (an understatement); that would mean not only losing healthy business and defense ties, but also being left to face the undivided attention and censure of much of the Third World and the United Nations. "If it were up to the UN we would be the second in line," Defense Minister Izhak Rabin said at the end of March 1987, explaining one reason for his opposition to sanctions against South Africa.

If these propositions are correct, we would expect Israeli–South African relations to be considerably more resistant to pressures for change in the status quo than the relations between other countries in the West and South Africa. And this is precisely what the events of summer 1985, reviewed at the end of chapter 10, demonstrate. It would seem that nothing short of some political *force majeure* can begin to loosen the Israeli–South African embrace, a conclusion that was further tested and born out by developments in 1986 and early 1987. It was in March 1987 that the Israeli government, fearing damage to its relations with Capitol Hill, found itself dragged kicking and screaming to the point of saying that it would not sign still more military contracts with South Africa—in the future. This great Israeli concession drew some immediate applause in the United States, and then the entire matter was dispatched to the memory hole.

In the summer of 1986, a troubling question came up in Israeli government circles: How much longer will the South African government be in power? The question had been asked before sporadically, but now it seemed to have some potential policy implications as well. A few pessimists, *Haaretz* reported, thought that Israel could not count on the government remaining white for much longer than five years. Others estimated it would be at least two or three times that long, and probably longer. At the same time Cameroon and a few other black African countries appeared close to re-establishing diplomatic relations with Israel, and questions were raised there as to whether the relationship with South Africa did not impede such a trend. Moreover, from a public relations standpoint, it was problematic for Israel to be seen as the last ally on unabashedly good terms with a racist, violent regime. Every single Western country, with the exception of Switzerland, which professes neutrality, had already imposed sanctions. American Jewish leaders also indicated that Israel's stance on South Africa was a matter of concern and was requiring extra effort to defend. Around these themes a school of thought formed in Israel which favored not only lower public visibility in the relations with Pretoria but indeed a reassessment of these relations. Dr. Yossi Beilin, director-general of the Foreign Ministry, became the main proponent of cooler Israeli–South African ties. Political scientist Shlomo Avineri, a former director-general of the Foreign Ministry himself, as well as Communications Minister Amnon Rubinstein, shared Beilin's sentiments on this issue.

But to call this view a school of thought is probably overgenerous. Virtually everyone else who counted in the Israeli establishment favored business as usual with the land of apartheid; Yossi Beilin's approach was derided as "moralistic," unsuitable for the harsh realities of this world. In fact, not even the other director-general of the Foreign Ministry, Avraham Tamir, sided with Beilin. As Roy Isacowitz of the *Jerusalem Post* pointed out, "Those in the government who oppose taking punitive measures against South Africa argue that the commercial and strategic repercussions of such actions could be grave while the benefits would be little more than symbolic."[1] A few in the government did favor tougher words towards South Africa, knowing that its government will not let mere rhetoric damage a vital relationship. But Gideon Pat, Minister of Science and Technology, was wary: "I will not suggest that we raise objections too hastily and identify with the protesters who are made up largely of people who say one thing and think something else."

In August, as South Africa was subject to the most severe international sanctions in its history, a high-level Israeli delegation went there to discuss an expansion of trade. Among the visiting officials were the director-general of the Finance Ministry and the state's chief scientist. An Israeli statement issued after the talks referred to gains leading to "mutual understanding of each other's economic problems and priorities." Suspicions increased that Israel, long thought "a weak link in the chain of international sanctions" as the *Financial Times* put it,[2] was prepared to serve as a lifeline for South Africa. Israel already serves as a way station for some South African exports and supplies South Africa with electronics, and military and nuclear technology.

Business continued as usual through the rest of 1986. In November it was revealed that Israel had sold South Africa at least two in-flight refueling tankers, a dramatic breakthrough that will enable the South African air force to strike and intervene virtually anywhere in Sub-Saharan Africa (chapter 6). The South Africa–Israel Chamber of Commerce reported that over the previous year South African exports to Israel leaped 70 percent. Exports to Israel of steel, which is embargoed by the United States, jumped 95 percent over the same period.[3] South African coal, also threatened by international sanctions, continued to flow to Israel on favorable terms.

At the end of 1986, the association of Israeli city governments sent a delegation to South Africa to study how municipalities there operate. And in the last week of December, it was reported in the British press that South Africa was planning to develop Marion Island, a remote Antarctic territory. Some experts feared the area might be used for nuclear tests. Israeli officers were seen there along with the South Africans (chapter 7).

Still, during all that time, the official stance of the government was that "Israel will not lag behind the Western world" in its steps against Pretoria. Prime Minister Shimon Peres said so on several occasions, even as Israel was lagging badly and no steps were being considered.

And what if at some point Israel should find itself under pressure so great that it is no longer enough just to say that Israel opposes apartheid totally and completely and unconditionally, etc.? In such a case, the government could be counted on to come up with a formula that "would have as little bite as possible while still creating a serious impression" (Diplomatic correspondent Benny Morris in the *Jerusalem Post*).[4]

Such a troublesome situation did arise in early 1987. Section 508 of the Comprehensive Anti-Apartheid Act passed by the United States Congress the previous fall over Ronald Reagan's objection[5] required the President to report to Congress "on the extent to which the international embargo on the sale and exports of arms and military technology to South Africa is being violated." The President was to identify the offending countries "with a view toward ending military assistance" to them. The provision apparently crept unwanted into the bill in the heat of anti-apartheid sentiment on Capitol Hill before Israel's friends and lobbyists had the chance to block it. Since the House accepted the Senate version of the bill, the House-Senate conference committee, where the provision might have been deleted, never convened.

Israeli officials immediately realized that that meant trouble, "a time bomb set to explode in April" when it was due. Although hardly anyone believed that United States military assistance to Israel—$1.8 billion a year and higher than to any other country—was in any danger, the matter did require attention.

At the end of January 1987, *Newsweek* magazine reported that Defense Minister Rabin had made a secret trip to Pretoria to explain the trouble on the horizon and the need to lower the profile. According to well placed sources, Rabin told the South Africans that "the alliance can continue but much more quietly."[6]

Trouble on the horizon or not, even as late as January 21, 1987, the *Jerusalem Post* reported that "Peres declined to commit the country to following the United States lead on sanctions," in apparent contradiction to his own earlier statements. All other senior government ministers remained adamantly opposed to any move to loosen the links with South Africa: Prime Minister Izhak Shamir; Rabin, who in 1976 invited Vorster to Jerusalem and extended him royal treatment; Ariel Sharon; Moshe Arens; and Ezer Weizmann. The last three are former defense ministers with long careers in defense and, naturally, extensive dealings with South Africa. Even debate on the issue was discouraged: Israeli newspaper editors were urged by government officials to "stay away from this sensitive matter of national interest."[7]

In January, Yossi Beilin attempted to organize a colloquium of ministry and extra-ministry experts on Israeli policy towards South Africa, but the forum was cancelled by acting Foreign Minister Ezer Weizmann. Beilin's efforts angered Rabin, who described him as an "elephant in a china shop" and complained to Peres. "Beilin will not be the one who determines the future of our relations with South Africa," Rabin vowed. Communications Minister Amnon Rubinstein, who was Beilin's only ally in the cabinet, said he was "deeply disappointed" that not a single Labor Party minister was on record as favoring any steps against South Africa. At the time Israeli officials had reason to hope that some understanding would be quietly reached with the U.S. Administration: Perhaps the government could say that it will not sign any *additional* contracts with South Africa and be allowed to continue the existing relationship, or another arrangement along these lines.

In February, Shamir repeated in Washington that his government had no intention to impose sanctions: "We keep our commitments," he declared. By then a few Israeli officials had coined the term "deprofilization" to refer to the need to proceed with even greater secrecy and lower public visibility. But that did not stop Tourism Minister Sharir from meeting with the South African Ambassador in mid-February to discuss ways to increase tourism "as a bridge to good relations" between Israel and South Africa. Toward the same end, Raphi Farber, director-general of the Tourism Ministry, received his South African counterpart and a delegation of white travel agents. The Israeli state-run radio was broadcasting commercials urging Israelis to "visit charming South Africa," to which all flights were booked solid for months in advance.

From late January until the beginning of April 1987, the Israeli and American press were flooded with reports about the extent of South African–Israeli relations. The reports often included overviews of the military relationship, as detailed in chapter 6 and in James Adams's *The Unnatural Alliance*. For the first time in history, the military relationship was forced into the open and Israeli officials were no longer in a position to dismiss what was sure to be stated in the forthcoming report to Congress. In a front page story on January 29 the *New York Times* reported that military officials were saying the relationship with South Africa involved "hundreds if not thousands of jobs in Israeli military industries and several hundred million dollars in earnings.'' The Israeli newspaper *Davar* cited a $500 million figure, while another report in the *New York Times* said the unofficial estimate was $400–$800 million (March 20).

Perhaps more than anything else, it was the conviction and life sentence in March to Jonathan Pollard, the Israeli-recruited spy in the United States, that complicated matters enough for the Israeli government to do something—or, more precisely, say something. "If we did not have the Pollard affair hanging over our heads, April 1 would not have looked so scary," the *New York Times* quoted a senior official. "But it was clear to everyone in the cabinet that there is no way now that anyone can fool around with the Americans." By then even Rabin and Shamir realized that the issue of South Africa would not go away, not after the acrimony over this latest scandal on top of Israel's role in the Iran-Contra affair. Under the circumstances, Prime Minister Shamir "understands that Israel must do something, with an eye on Washington, even if it is only a gesture of some kind," his aides said.[8] A gesture accompanied by a carefully worded statement about the future was definitely in order, many agreed: "Undoubtedly today we cannot take a stand which conflicts with the declared policy of the United States," warned an editorial in *Maariv*, adding that "this is a difficult job which will require the skills of a wordsmith."[9]

After a lengthy debate on March 18, the Israeli cabinet made the expected announcement that it would not sign additional contracts with South Africa "in the sphere of defense" and that it would limit Israel's cultural, official, and tourist relations with that country. The word "sanctions" cannot be found in the government statement. A committee would be set up and given two months, by which time this matter should no longer be in the limelight, to study possible steps in the above areas. Those were expected to range from the purely verbal to the symbolic. The cabinet finally got to debate the committee's proposals in July—and shelved them. Then, unexpectedly, some steps were announced on September 16. A *Maariv* headline two days later read: "Most Sanctions Imposed by Israel against S.A. are Meaningless."

It was immediately obvious that even if the "no additional military contracts" declaration was to be taken at face value, it is unverifiable, given the secrecy. It will instead be necessary to rely on the word of the Israeli government, which issued the statement under panic at five minutes to midnight—and which had given nearly identical assurances in 1977 after the United Nations embargo. More importantly, it is pure conjecture that in order to maintain their relationship Israel and South Africa need to sign any *new* contracts; the current ones may run until at least the 1990s, and some are likely to include automatic renewal clauses that would make new agreements unnecessary.

Military experts interviewed on Israeli radio on the day the government made the announcement said that the country's military industry will not be adversely affected, that is, the gesture will have no practical effect. The Israeli–South African relationship easily survived the Congressional report.

In London, the African National Congress spokesman told the *Jerusalem Post* that this relationship was so intimate that under numerous secret agreements Israel and South Africa must resupply each other with any arms they may be lacking.[10]

As Peres was telling the Knesset that Israel would limit its ties with Pretoria, his adviser Avraham Burg was in South Africa, ostensibly on a fund-raising mission. He may also have explained the Israeli government's announcement to officials there. Also in South Africa were Micha Inon, chairman of the Israeli Broadcasting Authority and Nathan Cohen, the Authority's legal adviser.

After the announcement, Israeli officials continued to express their frustration at being left with little choice but to say what they had, making it clear that they would have preferred to do nothing and say nothing. Rabin was still bitter: "Though the Defense Minister did not say so specifically, it was clear that if not for U.S. pressure he would be very much in favor of continuing the links with South Africa."[11] And as the *New York Times* reported:

Senior Israeli officials were blunt in indicating that this plan was directed first and foremost at the U.S. Congress, not South Africa. In devising it the cabinet was seeking a delicate balance of interests: the minimum amount of Israeli sanctions on South Africa, with the minimum negative effect on Israel's military exports in return for the maximum impact on Congress and American Jews.[12]

Eliahu Lankin, the former Israeli Ambassador in South Africa, thought that Israel should not sit still and at the very least, protest before the United States. In an article titled "U.S. Piper's Unfair South African Tune" he determined that the growing anti-apartheid sentiment in the

United States had to do with American politics, not with South Africa, where "there has been a very perceptible change" and "a new spirit." Thus in their pursuit of voters, the defeated Democrats "suddenly discovered a new horse to flog: apartheid in South Africa." Naturally, "the Republicans could not stand idly by and allow the Democrats to reap all the benefits from so convenient a cause," and hence the bipartisan sanctions. But the revolting thing is that "they seek to impose their political stand on other countries, using the weapon of economic support as a means of blackmail. . . . what moral right has America to exert pressure on Israel to participate in action against South Africa?" Though the former Israeli diplomat recognizes that "Israel has no alternative but to succumb to America's demands . . . that does not mean that we should not do so under protest."[13]

Predictably, the U.S. State Department said it welcomed the announcement of the Israeli government, "a positive development," according to spokesman Charles Redman. Representative Mickey Leland, former chairman of the Congressional Black Caucus, also praised the Israeli government and called its statement a "breakthrough."

The South African leadership's reaction was low-key, apparently so as to avoid unnecessary strains in the relationship at a difficult moment. The white government appreciated that under the circumstances Israel had no choice but to say what it had, and that the reluctant statement was the absolute minimum necessary to satisfy the U.S. Congress. Thus President Botha said that though he did not agree with Israel's decision he "sympathized with its position" as it feared "losing billions of dollars annually in American aid." It is the United States that should be blamed for doing the Kremlin's job, he said.[14] Foreign Minister Roelof Botha, who in the past often reacted angrily and with threats under similar circumstances, this time showed understanding and avoided public criticism of Israel. He too said that what happened was "clearly a direct result of pressure by the United States." Evidently, "the hope in Pretoria would be that the secrecy would enable Israel to extend current contracts and find loopholes in its embargo," South African commentators pointed out.[15]

The South African media was also understanding of Israel and directed its indignation at the United States. The *Transvaler* of March 20 described the United States as "the instigator which is bedeviling a working understanding between two smaller, but technologically speaking, phenomenally developing states." The South African

Broadcasting Company, in a commentary program that normally parallels government thinking, deplored "the international blackmail role—the bully boy tactics—that the United States Congress has now resorted to in its vendetta against South Africa."

The South African Jewish Board of Deputies declared that sanctions and disinvestment "undermine the ability to create conditions in which steps can be taken toward the achievement of an apartheid-free society." But it hoped that the Israeli action would still not undermine a relationship "based on deep-rooted religious and cultural affiliations."

In the United States, Israeli supporters came up with several creative justifications after they too could no longer deny what they had repeatedly denied for nearly two decades. The "everybody does it" and "Arab oil" themes (chapter 8) were still useful, but it was also argued that, well, maybe Israel did supply a few arms to South Africa but those were for external defense, not for the purpose of repressing the African majority: "Does anyone suggest," asked a March 27 editorial in the *Jewish Week*, echoing former Israeli Ambassador Izhak Unna, "that parts for jet fighters and submarines from Israel will be used against Black South Africans in the townships?" Evidently, Israel deserves praise for keeping the South African forces busy outside the townships. The *Jewish Week* editors left it unclear whether they would have rewritten the UN embargo resolution to cover only weapons that kill demonstrators—such as the Israeli Galil rifle and Uzi submachine gun. And did Israel violate the arms embargo? Well, how can a country such as Israel be in favor of embargoes? Another popular argument in publications with a similar orientation was that Israel must produce and export weapons "to survive," unlike others who are merely greedy; if Israel could, it would gladly sell weapons only to democratic countries but as things are in this world. . . . Besides, others said, it is good for the West if Israel helps secure the sea lanes around the Cape of Good Hope, and if Israel ends its relationship with South Africa, other countries will be glad to step in immediately. Anyway, South Africa does not even need Israeli weapons because it is militarily independent, and so on and so forth.

The report to Congress, prepared by the State Department Bureau of Intelligence and Research, covered only conventional weapons. The unclassified version said that Israel has regularly provided weapons systems and subsystems and technical assistance to South Africa, undisturbed by the UN arms embargo; the relationship has been continuous and on a government-to-government basis. Companies in France and Italy were also found to have violated the arms embargo; an early version of the report said that the French and Italian governments knew about the violations, but this was deleted from the final version, apparently for reasons of diplomacy. The two governments have denied knowledge of any such dealings. Under a third category of violations, private companies in Britain, West Germany, Switzerland and the Netherlands have sold South Africa military items "on occasion" or sold equipment considered in the gray area between military and civilian applications. This was said to have happened without government permission. Israeli officials were understandably pleased that other countries were mentioned in the report.

The extent of Israel's military relations with South Africa was outlined in the classified portion of the report. The Israeli press reported some of the highlights of this portion, such as Israel's training of South African forces in combat and counterinsurgency, its sharing with South Africa of information on Soviet equipment, and transfers of Israeli technology that enabled South Africa to build major weapons systems, that is, "its own" jet fighter, patrol ships, missiles, and electronic equipment. The classified version of the report also said that South Africa has established various dummy companies in Europe in order to facilitate the acquisition of those Israeli weapons that it is not licensed to produce locally.[16] *Haaretz* noted that other than for military equipment originating in the United States, Israel does not demand certification as to the final destination of shipments sold to private arms dealers ("end-user"). Since there is never a shortage of middlemen and dummy companies, this virtually guarantees that no matter what happens South Africa will continue to have access to its favorite Israeli weapons. Directly or not so directly, Israel will continue to lend a hand under varying levels of secrecy until the clock of apartheid ticks five minutes to midnight, and perhaps even a bit beyond. A week after the Israeli government issued its statement, satirist Ephraim Sidon wrote "A Letter to a Dear South African Friend" in *Maariv*. Though the literal translation cannot reflect the beauty of the piece in the original, the message remains timeless:

> You can oppress, discriminate, shoot Blacks
> Be racist—that's no tragedy

As long as the dead Black
Was shot by an Uzi round.

And if the head was split open with a club
Which was made in Israel
We will be the last ones in the world
To make a fuss over apartheid . . .

At times, as general lip service,
We'll condemn and say ''not very nice''
But better one Kfir in the hand
Than three speeches coming out of our mouth.

And the arms will flow
No, we will not stop.
This is signed
In black and white.

That's because we have a
Long-term policy:
Money has no smell
And certainly no color.

Anyway, my good friend
In Pretoria,
Over here economics
Is more desirable than history.

So don't be upset
And get ready
To continue business
Under the table.[17]

NOTES

1. *Jerusalem Post* overseas weekly edition, June 28, 1986.

2. *Financial Times*, August 6, 1986.

3. ''Israel's Support for South Africa Is Unchanged,'' *New York Newsday*, November 25, 1986.

4. *Jerusalem Post* overseas weekly edition, October 18, 1986.

5. The U.S. legislation included a ban on new investments, termination of landing rights for South African Airways, and a prohibition on flights to South Africa by U.S. civil aircraft. It further banned loans to the South Afri-

can government and private sector, prohibited imports of South African iron, steel and gold coins, affirmed the arms embargo and prohibited the sale of computers used by the military and police.

6. *Newsweek*, February 2, 1987, and the *Washington Post*, February 22, 1987, p. C2.

7. *Washington Post*, February 22, 1987, p. C2.

8. *Jerusalem Post*, March 18, 1987.

9. *Maariv*, March 16, 1987.

10. *Jerusalem Post*, March 19, 1987.

11. *Jerusalem Post*, April 1, 1987.

12. *New York Times*, March 20, 1987, p. A3.

13. *Jerusalem Post*, April 8, 1987.

14. *Jerusalem Post*, March 27, 1987.

15. *New York Times*, March 20, 1987, p. A3.

16. *Jerusalem Post*, April 2, 1987, and *Haaretz*, April 2, 1987.

17. *Maariv*, March 27, 1987.

Appendixes

APPENDIX A

Resolution 40/64 E (1985) of the United Nations General Assembly on Relations between Israel and South Africa.

RESOLUTION 40/64 E

Relations between Israel and South Africa

The General Assembly,

Reaffirming its resolutions on relations between Israel and South Africa,

Having considered the special report of the Special Committee against *Apartheid* on recent developments concerning relations between Israel and South Africa,[9]

Noting with appreciation the efforts of the Special Committee to expose the increasing and continuing collaboration between Israel and South Africa,

Reiterating that the increasing collaboration by Israel with the racist régime of South Africa, especially in the military and nuclear fields, in defiance of resolutions of the General Assembly and the Security Council is a serious hindrance to international action for the eradication of *apartheid*, an encouragement to the racist régime of South Africa to persist in its criminal policy of *apartheid* and a hostile act against the oppressed people of South Africa and the entire African continent and constitutes a threat to international peace and security,

1. *Commends* the Special Committee against *Apartheid* for publicizing the growing relations between Israel and South Africa and promoting public

[9] A/40/22/Add.2.

awareness of the grave dangers of the alliance between Israel and South Africa;

2. *Again strongly condemns* the continuing and increasing collaboration of Israel with the racist régime of South Africa, especially in the military and nuclear fields;

3. *Demands* that Israel desist from and terminate all forms of collaboration with South Africa forthwith, particularly in the military and nuclear fields, and abide scrupulously by the relevant resolutions of the General Assembly and the Security Council;

4. *Calls upon* all Governments and organizations in a position to do so to exert their influence to persuade Israel to desist from such collaboration;

5. *Requests* the Special Committee to continue to publicize, as widely as possible, information on the relations between Israel and South Africa;

6. *Again requests* the Secretary-General to render, through the Department of Public Information and the Centre against *Apartheid* of the Secretariat, all possible assistance to the Special Committee in disseminating information relating to the collaboration between Israel and South Africa;

7. *Further requests* the Special Committee to keep the matter under constant review and to report to the General Assembly and the Security Council as appropriate.

The resolution was adopted by 102 votes to 20, with 30 abstentions (resolution 40/64 E)

In favour: Afghanistan, Albania, Algeria, Angola, Argentina, Bahrain, Bangladesh, Benin, Bhutan, Bolivia, Botswana, Brazil, Bunei Darussalam, Bulgaria, Burkina Faso, Burundi, Byelorussia SSR, Cape Verde, Central African Republic, Chad, China, Comoros, Congo, Cuba, Cyprus, Czechoslovakia, Democratic Kampuchea, Democratic Yemen, Djibouti, Ecuador, Egypt, Ethiopia, Gabon, Gambia, German Democratic Republic, Ghana, Guinea, Guinea-Bissau, Guyana, Haiti, Hungary, India, Indonesia, Iran, Iraq, Jordan, Kenya, Kuwait, Lao People's Democratic Republic, Lebanon, Lesotho, Libyan Arab Jamahiriya, Madagascar, Malaysia, Maldives, Mali, Malta, Mauritania, Mauritius, Mexico, Mongolia, Morocco, Mozambique, Nicaragua, Niger, Nigeria, Oman, Pakistan, Papua New Guinea, Peru, Philippines, Poland, Qatar, Romania, Rwanda, Sao Tome and Principe, Saudi Arabia, Senegal, Seychelles, Sierra Leone, Singapore, Somalia, Sri Lanka, Sudan, Suriname, Syrian Arab Republic, Thailand, Togo, Tunisia, Turkey, Uganda, Ukrainian SSR, Union of Soviet Socialist Republics, United Arab Emirates, United Republic of Tanzania, Vanuatu, Venezuela, Viet Nam, Yemen, Yugoslavia, Zambia, Zimbabwe.

Against: Australia, Austria, Belgium, Canada, Denmark, Finland, France, Federal Republic of Germany, Grenada, Iceland, Ireland, Israel, Italy, Luxembourg, Netherlands, New Zealand, Norway, Sweden, United Kingdom, United States.

Abstaining: Bahamas, Barbados, Belize, Burma, Cameroon, Chile, Colombia, Costa Rica, Dominican Republic, Equatorial Guinea, Fiji, Greece, Guatemala, Honduras, Ivory Coast, Jamaica, Japan, Liberia, Malawi, Nepal, Panama, Portugal, Saint Lucia, Saint Vincent and the Grenadines, Samoa, Solomon Islands, Spain, Swaziland, Uruguay, Zaire.

Absent: Antigua and Barbuda, Dominica, El Salvador, Paraguay, St. Christopher and Nevis, Trinidad and Tobago.

APPENDIX B

Israel's Stance on UN General Assembly Resolutions Regarding South Africa in Recent Years.

(*All votes boycotted unless otherwise noted*)

1981

36/172A December 17: Situation in South Africa.

36/172B December 17: International Year of Mobilization Against South Africa.

36/172C December 17: Acts of Aggression by the Apartheid Regime Against Angola and Other Independent States.

36/172D December 17: Comprehensive and Mandatory Sanctions Against South Africa.

36/172E December 17: Military and Nuclear Collaboration with South Africa.

36/172F December 17: Arms Embargo Against South Africa.

36/172G December 17: Oil Embargo Against South Africa.

36/172H December 17: International Conference of Trade Unions on Sanctions Against South Africa.

36/172I December 17: Academic, Cultural and Sports Boycotts of South Africa.

36/172J December 17: Political Prisoners in South Africa. (Adopted without a vote.)

36/172K December 17: Women and Children Under Apartheid.

36/172L December 17; Public Information and Public Action Against Apartheid and Role of the Mass Media in the Struggle Against Apartheid.

36/172M December 17: RELATIONS BETWEEN ISRAEL AND SOUTH AFRICA.

36/172N December 17: Programme of Work of the Special Committee Against Apartheid.

36/172O December 17: Investments in South Africa.
36/172P December 17: United Nations Trust Fund for South Africa.

1982

37/1 October 21: Appeal for Clemency in Favour of South African Freedom Fighters.
37/2 October 21: South Africa's Application for Credit from the International Monetary Fund.
37/68 December 7: Further Appeal for Clemency in Favour of South Africa's Freedom Fighters.
37/69A December 9: Situation in South Africa.
37/69B December 9: Concerted International Action for the Elimination of Apartheid.
37/69C December 9: Comprehensive and Mandatory Sanctions Against South Africa.
37/69D December 9: Military and Nuclear Collaboration with South Africa.
37/69E December 9: Programme of Work of the Special Committee Against Apartheid.
37/69F December 9: RELATIONS BETWEEN ISRAEL AND SOUTH AF-RICA.
37/69G December 9: Apartheid in Sports.
37/69H December 9: Investments in South Africa.
37/69I December 9: United Nations Trust Fund for South Africa.
37/69J December 9: Oil Embargo Against South Africa.
37/101 December 14: Invasion of Lesotho by South Africa.

1983

38/11 November 15: Proposed New Racial Constitution of South Africa.
38/39A December 5: Situation in South Africa.
38/39B December 5: Programme of Action Against Apartheid.
38/39C December 5: Effects of Apartheid on the Countries of Southern Africa.
38/39D December 5: Sanctions Against South Africa.
38/39E December 5: Programme of Work of the Special Committee Against Apartheid.
38/39F December 5: RELATIONS BETWEEN ISRAEL AND SOUTH AF-RICA.
38/39G December 5: Military and Nuclear Collaboration with South Africa.
38/39H December 5: United Nations Trust Fund for South Africa.
38/39I December 5: Investments in South Africa.
38/39J December 5: Oil Embargo Against South Africa.
38/39K December 5: Apartheid in Sports.

1984

39/2 September 28: Situation in South Africa.

39/72A December 13: Comprehensive Sanctions Against the Apartheid Regime and Support to the Liberation Struggle in South Africa.

39/72B December 13: Programme of Work of the Special Committee Against Apartheid.

39/72C December 13: RELATIONS BETWEEN ISRAEL AND SOUTH AFRICA - VOTED AGAINST.

39/72D December 13: Apartheid in Sports.

39/72E December 13: Public Information and Public Action Against Apartheid.

39/72F December 13: United Nations Trust Fund for South Africa. (Adopted without a vote.)

39/72G December 13: Concerted International Action for the Elimination of Apartheid.

1985

40/64A December 10: Comprehensive Sanctions Against the Racist Regime of South Africa - AGAINST

40/64B December 10: Situation in South Africa and Assistance to the Liberation Movement - ABSTAINED

40/64C December 10: World Conference on Sanctions Against Racist South Africa - ABSTAINED

40/64D December 10: Public Information and Public Action Against *Apartheid* - ABSTAINED

40/64E December 10: Relations Between Israel and South Africa - AGAINST

40/64F December 10: Programme of Work of the Special Committee Against *Apartheid* - ABSTAINED

40/64G December 10: International Convention Against *Apartheid* in Sports - IN FAVOR

40/64H December 10: United Nations Trust Fund for South Africa - No Vote Taken.

40/64I December 10: Concerted International Action for the Elimination of *Apartheid* - ABSTAINED

Chronology: Milestones in Israeli–South African Relations

1948 South Africa is among the first countries to recognize the newly established State of Israel.

1953 South African Premier Daniel F. Malan is the first head of a foreign government to visit Israel.

1961 Israeli–South African relations deteriorate as Israel joins the anti-apartheid censure initiative in the United Nations General Assembly.

1967 The Israeli victory in the June war heralds the beginning of a thaw with an admiring South African government.

1971 Israel offers a financial contribution to the Organization of African Unity. The contribution is rejected but the post-1967 thaw with Pretoria nonetheless suffers a temporary setback.

1973 The October war and black Africa's break with Israel mark a turning point in relations with South Africa, which become increasingly cozy.

1974 Israel upgrades its diplomatic representation in South Africa to the level of an embassy. The move is reciprocated the following year.

1976 Prime Minister John Vorster visits Israel and signs agreements for significant cooperation. The "historic breakthrough" is widely applauded in South Africa.

1977 Menachem Begin, former head of the Israeli–South African Friendship League, takes office as Prime Minister.

1978 Israeli Treasury Minister Simcha Erlich visits Pretoria in February and proposes that South Africa use Israel as a stepping-stone to Western markets.

1979 A mysterious flash in the Indian Ocean is suspected of being the result of a South African–Israeli nuclear test.

1985 In September, Israeli Foreign Minister Izhak Shamir tells the Conference of Presidents of Major American Jewish Organizations that Israel does not intend to change the character of its relations with South Africa.

1987 In March the Israeli government announces that it will not sign additional military contracts with South Africa. The announcement is made eleven days before a U.S. State Department report names Israel a major government-to-government arms ally of Pretoria.

Bibliography

ISRAEL AND SOUTH AFRICA

Abu-Lughod, Ibrahim, and Baha Abu Laban. *Settler Regimes in Africa and the Arab World: The Illusion of Endurance*. Wilmette, Ill.,: Medina University Press International, 1974.

Adam, Heribert. "Ethnic Politics and Crisis Management: Comparing South Africa and Israel." *Journal of Asian and African Studies* 18, nos. 1–2. (1983).

Adams, James. *The Unnatural Alliance*. London: Quartet Books, 1984.

Adelman, Kenneth. "Israel/South Africa: The Club of Pariahs." *Africa Report* (November–December 1980).

African Research Group. "David and Goliath Collaborate in Africa." *Leviathan* (September 1969).

Ainslee, Rosalynde. "Israel and South Africa: An Unlikely Alliance?" United Nations Department of Political and Security Affairs, Publication No. 81-18876, (1981).

Ajami, Fouad, and Martin H. Sours. "Israel and Sub-Saharan Africa: A Study of Interaction." *African Studies Review* 13, no. 3 (December 1970).

Arkin, Marcus. "South Africa, Its Jews and the Israel Connection." *South Africa International* (October 1977).

Astrakhov, S. "Alliance Between Tel Aviv and Pretoria." *International Affairs* (Moscow), no. 8 (August 1977).

Bandler, Kenneth, and George E. Gruen. "Israel and South Africa." A Special Report of the International Relations Department, The American Jewish Committee, (1985).

Barclay, Glen St. John. "Strategy of Despair: South Africa and the Alignment of the Alienated." *Journal for Contemporary History and International Relations* (South Africa) 7, no. 2 (December 1982).

Beit-Hallahmi, Benjamin. *The Israeli Connection: Who Israel Arms and Why*. New York: Pantheon, 1987.

———. "South Africa and Israel's Strategy of Survival." *New Outlook: Middle East Monthly* 20:54 (April–May 1977).

———. "Israel and South Africa 1977–1982: Business as Usual—and More." *New Outlook: Middle East Monthly* (February 1983).

Benabdallah, Abdelkader. *L'alliance raciste israelo-sud-africaine: Israel et les peuples noirs*. Montreal: Editions Canada-monde-arabe, 1979.

Bergman, Ernst. "South Africa and Israel: Different Countries with Common Problems." Johannesburg: South African Institute of International Affairs (1968).

Bernstein, Edgar. "Israel, the OAU and South Africa." *Jewish Affairs* (South Africa, July 1971).

Blow, Desmond. *Take Now Thy Son: The Yom Kippur War, South Africa's Involvement*. Cape Town: Howard Timmins, 1974.

Bollag, Mitchel. "South Africa and Israel: A Comparative Study in Settler-Colonialism." Unpublished paper, City College of the City University of New York, 1975.

Branaman, Brenda. "South African-Israeli Relations."Congressional Service Report No. 81-174F (Washington, D.C.) (July 30, 1981).

Brytenbach, Willie. "Isolation and Cooperation." *Africa Report* (November–December, 1980).

Bullier, Antoine. "Les relations entre l'Afrique du Sud et Israel" *Revue francaise d'etudes politiques africaines* (November 1975).

Bunzl, John. *Die Vereinigten Staaten, Israel and Sudafrika: eine Untersuchung ihrer Beziehungen*. (Wien:Braumuller; Laxenburg: Austrian Institute for International Affairs, 1981).

Burnett, Nicholas R. "The Israel–South Africa Connection: Dangerous Bedfellows." *The Nation* (May 20, 1978).

Calloway, J. G. "Israel and South Africa: Unity in Isolation." *Middle East International* (January 1978).

Cave, Sarah. "Israel and South Africa: Zionism and Apartheid." *Arab Affairs* (London, Winter 1986–1987).

Chazan, Naomi. "The Fallacies of Pragmatism: Israeli Foreign Policy towards South Africa." *African Affairs* (April 1983).

Collins, Carole. "Israel–South Africa Ties Probed." *National Catholic Reporter* (January 22, 1982).

Curtis, Michael. "Israel and South Africa." *Middle East Review* Special Report (October 1983).

Executive Office of the President, Office of Science and Technology Policy. "Ad Hoc Panel Report on the September 22 Event." (Washington, D.C., July 15, 1980).

Farley, Deborah, and T. Lawrence. "Israel and South Africa: Parallels and Linkages." A paper presented to the annual meeting of the Middle East Studies Association, New York, 1977.

Farsoun, Samih. "South Africa and Israel: A Special Relationship." United Nations African Institute for Economic Development and Planning, Dakar, 1975.

The Financial Mail (South Africa) "Israel: A Survey." 50 page supplement (May 11, 1984).

Finger, Seymour M. "Israel and South Africa." *Encore* (April 4, 1977).

Fitzgerald, Patrick, and Jonathan Bloch. "Alliance Among Outlaws." *The Middle East* (London, May 1983).

Goell, Yosef. "A View from Jerusalem." *Africa Report*, (November–December 1980).

Goldfield, Steve. *Garrison State: Israel's Role in U.S. Global Strategy*. San Francisco: Palestine Focus Publications, 1985.

Goldfield, Steve, and Hilton Obenzinger. "South Africa: The Israeli Connection." *American-Arab Affairs* (Fall 1986).

Goodman, Hirsh. "Parallel Illusions." *The Jerusalem Post Magazine* (September 11, 1981).

Harris, Brice. "The South Africanization of Israel." *Arab Studies Quarterly* (Summer 1984).

Hauser, Rita. "Israel, South Africa and the West." *Washington Quarterly* (Summer 1979).

Hellyer, Peter. *Israel and South Africa: Development of Relations, 1967–1974*. London: Palestine Action, 1975.

Hunter, Jane. *Israeli Foreign Policy: South Africa and Central America*. Boston: South End Press, 1987.

———. *Undercutting Sanctions: Israel, the U.S. and South Africa*. Washington, D.C.: Washington Middle East Associates, 1986.

———. "Israel and the Bantustans." *The Journal of Palestine Studies* (Spring 1986).

———. "Israel and South Africa: How Close?" *Israeli Foreign Affairs* (United States, February 1985).

Husain, Azim. "The West, South Africa and Israel: A Strategic Triangle." *Third World Quarterly* 4, no. 1, (1982).

Ibrahim, Omar. "Israel-South Africa Entente." *Mainstream* (October 23, 1976).

Isacowitz, Roy. "Twinning with a Tyrant." *The Jerusalem Post Magazine* (November 9, 1984).

Israel Government Press Bulletin. "Reply by Prime Minister David Ben-Gurion to Motions on the Voting of Israel's Delegation to the United Nations on the Question of South Africa's Apartheid Policy in the Knesset." (November 27, 1961).

Israel Mission to the United Nations. "Statement on Apartheid in the Special Political Committee by Ambassador Arieh Eshel." (November 1, 1961).

Jabbour, George. *Settler Colonialism in Southern Africa and the Middle East.* Khartoum: University of Khartoum, 1970.

Jacobson, Kenneth. "Israel and South Africa." *Israel Economist* (December 19, 1979).

Kagedan, Allan. "Fallacies about Israel's Ties with South Africa." American Jewish Committee, Institute of Human Relations, 1985.

Kashin, Y. "Zionist-Racist Alliance." *International Affairs* (Moscow, April 1975).

Kearney, Vincent S. "Israel and South Africa: Strange Alliance." *America* 135 (September 25, 1976).

Keller, Gerald (Major, USMC). "Israeli–South African Trade: An Analysis of Recent Developments." *Naval War College Review* (Spring 1978).

Koch, Edward. "Double Standard Where Israel Is Concerned." *Jewish Press* (January 18, 1985).

Kramish, Arnold. "Nuclear Flashes in the Night." *Washington Quarterly* (Summer 1980).

Kreindler, Joshua David. "South Africa, Jewish Palestine and Israel: The Growing Relationship 1919–1974." *African Quarterly* (India), 20 (3–4) (1981).

Lapid, Yosef. "Lemaan D'rom Africa Lo Echeshe." ("For the Sake of South Africa I Shall Not Keep My Silence.") *Maariv* (March 14, 1974).

Lee, Richard. "Ethnicity, Militarism and Human Rights—Israel and South Africa." *Dialectical Anthropology* 8, nos. 1–2 (1983).

Lewis, Flora. "Pretoria's Israel Mask." *New York Times* (January 28, 1983).

Madison Area Committee on Southern Africa. "Israel and South Africa." (Madison, Wis., 1971).

Manning, Robert. "South Africa–Israel Connections—But Is the U.S. Pleased?" *African Development* 10 (London, October 1976).

Manning, Robert, and Stephen Talbot. "White House Nuclear Report: What's in the Clouds? (Mystery Flash off South Africa.)" *New West* (June 2, 1980).

———. "American Cover-up on Israeli Bomb." *The Middle East* (London, June 1980).

Mansour, Christopher, and Richard P. Stevens. *Internal Control in Israel and South Africa: The Mechanisms of Colonial-Settler Regimes.* London: The International Organisation for the Elimination of All Forms of Racial Discrimination, March 1983.

Marmon, Lucretia. "Israel and South Africa: The Odd Couple." *Times of Israel and World Jewish Review* (June 1974).

Mazrui, Ali A. "Zionism and Apartheid: Strange Bedfellows or Natural Allies?" *Alternatives* no. 9 (Summer 1983).

McTague, John J. "Israel and South Africa: A Comparison of Policies." *Journal of Palestine Studies* (Spring 1985).

Moleah, Alfred T. *Israel and South Africa*. London: The International Organisation for the Elimination of All Forms of Racial Discrimination, 1979.

———. "Israel and South Africa: The Special Relationship." *Africa Report* (November–December 1980).

———. "Violations of Palestinian Human Rights: South African Parallels." *Journal of Palestine Studies* 10, no. 2 (1981).

Ohaegbulam, Ogboaja F. "South Africa and Israel in the Context of Southern African Politics." *The Western Journal of Black Studies* (Spring 1979).

Ojo, Olusola. "Israeli–South African Connections and Afro-Israeli Relations." *International Studies* (January–March, 1982).

Osia, Kunirum. *Israel, South Africa and Black Africa*. New York: University Press of America, 1981.

———. "Israel–South Africa Connection: Cause or Consequence of Black African Middle East Policy." *Search: Journal for Arab and Islamic Studies* 2(3–4) (1981).

Peled, Ruth. "Bilateral Trade Between South Africa and Israel, Theory and Practice." Johannesburg: University of Witwatersrand, MBA Thesis, 1982.

Penn, Jack. "South Africa/Israel Cooperation in War." *Armed Forces* (South Africa, February 1981).

Penycat, John. "Was It the Bomb?" *New African* (June 1980).

Santis, Yitzhak. "Israel and South Africa: A Lie Well Told." *Israel Horizons* (January 1980).

Segev, Shmuel. "Israel Umedinot Hehasut." ("Israel and the Homelands.") *Maariv* (December 2, 1983).

Shaham, David. "Both Wrong and Stupid." *New Outlook: Middle East Monthly* (September–October 1976).

Shapiro, Zalman "A Study of Some of the Factors Influencing the Use of Israel as a Springboard for South African Exports." Graduate School of Business, University of Cape Town, 1979.

Shaw, Timothy. "Oil, Israel and the OAU: The Political Economy of Energy in Southern Africa." *Africa Report* (January–March, 1976).

Simon, Leslie D. "Israel and South Africa: The Allegations and the Reality." Institute for Jewish Policy Planning and Research of the Synagogue Council of America, 1980.

Stevens, Richard P., and Abdelwahab M. Elmessiri. *Israel and South Africa: The Progression of a Relationship*. New York: New World Press, 1976.

Stevens, Richard P. "Smuts and Weizmann." *Journal of Palestine Studies* 3(1) (1973).

———. "Zionism, South Africa and Apartheid: The Paradoxical Triangle." *Phylon* no. 2 (Summer 1971).

Tomarkin, Mordechai. "Yachasei Israel–Drom Africa Baespaclaria Shel Istrategiat Mediniut Hahutz Shel Israel." ("The Israeli–South African Relationship as Reflected in the Looking Glass of Israeli Foreign Policy Strategy.") *Skira Hodshit*, A Monthly Journal for IDF Officers (December 1980).

Tomeh, George. *Israel and South Africa: The Unholy Alliance.* New York: New World Press, 1973.

United Nations Centre Against Apartheid. "Alliance Between South Africa and Israel: Statements at the International Conference on the Alliance Between South Africa and Israel in Vienna, July 11–13, 1983." (New York, February 1984).

———. "Relations Between Israel and South Africa." *Notes and Documents* (New York, February 1977).

United Nations General Assembly. "First Special Report of the Special Committee Against Apartheid: Recent Developments Concerning Relations Between Israel and South Africa." (New York, September 17, 1981).

Unna, I. "Israel and South Africa—An Impressive Relationship" (Address by Israeli Ambassador I. Unna). *Zionist Record and South African Jewish Chronicle* (May 20, 1976).

Wade, Michael. "Bypassing Africa and History." *New Outlook: Middle East Monthly* (November 1976).

Weyl, Nathaniel. "Israel and South Africa: Two Beleaguered Elites." *Mankind Quarterly* 13, no. 3 (Great Britain, 1973).

SOUTH AFRICA

Adam, Heribert. *Modernizing Racial Discrimination: South Africa's Political Dynamics.* Berkeley: University of California Press, 1971.

Adam, Heribert, and Herman Giliomee. *Ethnic Power Mobilized: Can South Africa Change?* New Haven: Yale University Press, 1979.

Adelman, Kenneth. *Impact upon U.S. Security of a South African Nuclear Weapons Capability.* Arlington, Va.: SRI International, 1981.

Arkin, Marcus, ed. *South African Jewry: A Contemporary Survey.* Cape Town: Oxford University Press, 1984.

Barber, James. *The West and South Africa.* London: Royal Institute of International Affairs, 1982.

———. *South Africa's Foreign Policy 1945–1970.* New York: Oxford University Press, 1973.

Belfiglio, V. J. "The Cape Sea Route." *International Problems* (Fall 1980).

Bernstein, Edgar. *The Legacy of General Smuts: Its Significance for South Africa and the World*. Johannesburg: Eagle Press, 1950.

Brotz, Howard. *The Politics of South Africa: Democracy and Racial Diversity*. New York: Oxford University Press, 1977.

Brown, Douglas. *Against the World: A Study of White South African Attitudes*. London: William Collins & Sons, 1976.

Cervenka, Zdenek, and Barbara Rogers. *The Nuclear Axis: Secret Collaboration Between West Germany and South Africa*. New York: Times Books, 1978.

Chambati, A. "South Africa in the World: Political and Strategic Realities." The South African Institute of International Affairs (Johannesburg, 1976).

Cockram, Gail-Maryse. *Vorster's Foreign Policy*. Pretoria: Academica, 1970.

Conrad, Thomas. "Legal Arms for Apartheid." *The Nation* (January 21, 1984).

Crapanzano, Vincent. *Waiting: The Whites of South Africa*. New York: Random House, 1985.

Crocker, Chester. *South Africa's Defense Posture: Coping with Vulnerability*. Published for the Center for Strategic and International Studies at Georgetown University by Sage Publishers, 1981.

Decter, Moshe. "Arms Traffic with South Africa: Who Is Guilty?" The American Jewish Congress, New York, November 1976.

————. "South Africa and Black Africa: A Report on Growing Trade Relations." The American Jewish Congress, New York, August 1976.

Department of Defence, Republic of South Africa. "White Paper on Defence and Armament Production." 1973.

Department of Political and Security Council Affairs, United Nations Centre for Disarmament. Report of the Secretary-General. "South Africa's Plan and Capability in the Nuclear Field." New York, 1981.

De St. Jorre, John. *A House Divided: South Africa's Uncertain Future*. New York: Carnegie Endowment for International Peace, 1977.

Feit, E. "Community in a Quandary: The South African Jewish Community and Apartheid." *Race* 8(4) (April 1967).

Fisher, John. *The Afrikaners*. London: Cassel & Co., 1969.

Fitzsimons, Pat. *Arms for Apartheid: British Military Collaboration with South Africa*. London: Christian Concern for South Africa, 1981.

Frankel, Philip. *Pretoria's Praetorians: Civil-Military Relations in South Africa*. New York: Cambridge University Press, 1984.

Frederickson, George M. *White Supremacy: A Comparative Study in American and South African History*. New York: Oxford University Press, 1981.

Geldenhuys, Deon. *The Diplomacy of Isolation: South African Foreign Policy Making*. New York: St. Martin's Press, 1984.

————. *The Neutral Option and Subcontinental Solidarity*. Braamfontein: South African Institute of International Affairs, 1979.

————. *Some Foreign Policy Implications of South Africa's Total National Strategy*. Braamfontein: South African Institute of International Affairs, 1981.

Geller, David. "The Jewish Community of South Africa." A Background Memorandum, International Relations Department, The American Jewish Committee, May 1985.

Giniewski, Paul. *The Two Faces of Apartheid*. Chicago: Regner, 1965.

Greenberg, Stanley. *Race and State in Capitalist Development: Comparative Perspectives*. New Haven: Yale University Press, 1980.

Harrison, David. *The White Tribe of Africa*. Berkeley: University of California Press, 1982.

Hepple, Alexander. *South Africa: A Political and Economic History*. London: Pall Mall, 1967.

————. *South Africa: Workers Under Apartheid*. London: Published for The International Defense and Aid Fund by Christian Action Publications, Ltd., 1971.

Hiemstra, Rudolph Christian. *The Strategic Significance of Southern Africa*. Cape Town: Tafelberguitgewers, 1970.

Hough, M. "The Political Implication of the Possession of Nuclear Weapons for South Africa." *Strategy Review*, Institute for Strategic Studies, University of Pretoria, May 1980.

International Defence and Aid Fund. *The Apartheid War Machine*. London, 1980.

Isacowitz, Roy, and David Richardson. "Apartheid as a Jewish Problem." *The Jerusalem Post Magazine* (March 29, 1985).

Jacobson, Dan. "The Jews of South Africa: Portrait of a Flourishing Community." *Commentary* (January 1957).

Jacobson, Dan, and Ronald Segal. "Apartheid and South African Jewry: An Exchange." *Commentary* (November 1957).

Jaster, Robert. *South Africa's Narrowing Security Options*. London: International Institute for Strategic Studies, 1980.

Johnson, R. W. *How Long Will South Africa Survive?* London: Macmillan, 1977.

Katzew, Henry. "Jews in the Land of Apartheid." *Midstream* (December 1962).

Kirschmer, N. "Zionism and the Union of South Africa: Fifty Years of Friendship and Understanding." *Jewish Affairs* (South Africa, May 1960).

Korner, Peter. *Sudafrika zwischen Isolation und Kooperation: okonomische, politische und militarische Zusammenarbeit des Apartheidstaates mit*

Submetropolen (Brasilien, Argentinien, Iran, Israel, Taiwan, Sudkorea). Hamburg: Institut fur Afrika-Kunde, 1981.

Leonard, Richard. *South Africa at War: White Power and the Crisis in Southern Africa*. Westport, Conn.: Lawrence Hill & Co., 1983.

MacCrone, Ian Douglas. *Race Attitudes in South Africa: Historical, Experimental and Psychological Studies*. London: Oxford University Press, 1937.

Marquard, Leo. *The Peoples and Policies of South Africa*. New York: Oxford University Press, 1969.

McEwan, Christopher. *The Soviet Union and the Conventional Threat to South Africa*. Johannesburg: South African Institute of International Affairs, 1976.

Metrowich, F. R. *South Africa's New Frontiers*. Sandton: Valiant, 1977.

Moodie, T. Dunbar. *The Rise of Afrikanerdom: Power, Apartheid and the Afrikaner Civil Religion*. Berkeley: University of California Press, 1975.

Moolman, Henry Martin. *How They Hate Us: South Africa, and in Particular the Afrikaners, Their Church, Culture and Leaders Under Fire in the World Press*. Pretoria: Voortrekkerpers, 1965.

Mugomba, Agrippah T. *The Foreign Policy of Despair*. Kampala, Nairobi and Dar Es-Salaam: East African Literature Bureau, 1977.

North, James. *Freedom Rising: War and Peace in Southern Africa*. New York: Macmillan, 1985.

Patterson, Sheila. *The Last Trek: A Study of the Boer People and the Afrikaner Nation*. London: Routledge & Paul, 1957.

Penn, Jack. "Was It an Atomic Bomb or Was It a Flash of Inventive Animosity? A South African Point of View." *Armed Forces* (South Africa, April 1980).

Republic of South Africa. *South Africa Yearbook*. Johannesburg: The Information Service of South Africa, 1977.

Ridgeway, James. "Reagan's Secret Aid to Apartheid." *The Village Voice* (December 25, 1984).

Roberts, Michael, and A.E.G. Trollip. *The South African Opposition 1939–1945*. London: Longmans, Green & Co., 1947.

Rubin, Leslie. "Dialog: South African Jewry and Apartheid." *Africa Report* (February 1970).

Saron, Gustav, and Lois Hotz. *The Jews in South Africa*. Cape Town: Oxford University Press, 1955.

Shaw, Timothy. "Southern Africa: Co-operation and Conflict in an International Sub-System." *The Journal of Modern African Studies* 12 (4) (1974).

Shimoni, Gideon. *Jews and Zionism: The South African Experience 1910–1967*. Cape Town: Oxford University Press, 1980.

South Africa Parliament. *House of Assembly Debates*. Cape Town, 1973–1983.

Spence, J. E. "South Africa: The Nuclear Option," *African Affairs*, no. 80 (October 1981).

Starcke, Anna. *Survival*. Cape Town: Tafelberg Publishers, 1978.

Steinhart, Edward. "Shylock and Prospero: Antisemitism and Zionism in South African Ideology." [N.p.], (1974).

Steward, Alexander. *The World, the West and Pretoria*. New York: David McKay Co., 1978.

Study Commission on United States Policy Toward Southern Africa. *South Africa: Time Running Out*. Berkeley: University of California Press, 1981.

Thompson, Leonard, and Andrew Prior. *South African Politics*. New Haven: Yale, 1982.

United Nations General Assembly. Report of the Secretary General. "Implementation of the Declaration on the Denuclearization of Africa." Document #A/35/402, (September 1980).

United States House of Representatives. International Relations Committee, Subcommittee on Africa. "U.S.-South African Relations: Arms Embargo Implementation." Testimony by Sean Gervasi, H 461-74.1, July 14, 1977.

Van den Berghe, Pierre. *South Africa: A Study in Conflict*. Middletown, Conn.: Wesleyan University Press, 1965.

Vandenbosch, Amry. *South Africa and the World: The Foreign Policy of Apartheid*. Lexington: University Press of Kentucky, 1970.

Van-Rensburg, W. C. J. *South Africa's Strategic Minerals*. Johannesburg: Foreign Affairs Association, 1977.

Villiers, Les de. *South Africa: A Skunk Among Nations*. London: International Books, 1975.

Walker, Martin. "Apartheid's Secret Friends," *Africa* (November 1974).

The Washington Office on Africa Educational Fund. The September 22, 1979 Mystery Flash: Did South Africa Detonate a Nuclear Bomb? Washington, D.C., 1985.

Weisbord, Robert G. "The Dilemma of South African Jewry." *The Journal of Modern African Studies*, no. 2, (1967).

Wilson, Monica (Hunter), and Leonard Thompson. *The Oxford History of South Africa*. New York: Oxford University Press, 1971.

ISRAEL

Avineri, Shlomo. *Israel and the Palestinians*. New York: St. Martin's Press, 1971.

Begin, Menachem. *The Revolt*. Los Angeles: Nash Publishing, 1972.

Brecher, Michael. *The Foreign Policy System of Israel*. New Haven: Yale University Press, 1974.

———. *Decisions in Israel's Foreign Policy*. New Haven: Yale University Press, 1975.

———. "A Critique of Israel's Foreign Policy." *New Outlook: Middle East Monthly* (June 1973).

Chazan, Naomi. "Israel in Africa." *Jerusalem Quarterly* (Winter 1981).

Chomsky, Noam. *The Fateful Triangle: The United States, Israel and the Palestinians*. Boston: South End Press, 1983.

Curtis, Michael, and Susan A. Gitelson, eds. *Israel in the Third World*. New Brunswick: Transaction Books, 1976.

Curtis, Michael. "Africa, Israel and the Middle East." *Middle East Review* (Summer 1985).

Davenport, Elaine, Paul Eddy, and Peter Gilman. *The Plumbat Affair*. London: Futura Publications, 1978.

Davis, Leonard J. *Myths and Facts: A Concise Record of the Arab-Israeli Conflict*. Washington, D.C.: Near East Research, 1985.

Dowty, Alan. "Nuclear Proliferation: The Israeli Case." *International Studies Quarterly* (March 1978).

———. "Israel and Nuclear Weapons." *Midstream: A Monthly Jewish Review* (November 1976).

Eban, Abba. *The Story of Modern Israel*. New York: Random House, 1972.

El-Asmar, Fouzi. *To Be an Arab in Israel*. London: Frances Pinter Publishers, Ltd., 1975.

Elon, Amos. *The Israelis: Founders and Sons*. New York: Holt, Rinehart and Winston, 1971.

Feldman, Shai. *Israeli Nuclear Deterrence: A Strategy for the 1980's*. New York: Columbia University Press, 1982.

Gouldman, M. D. *Israel Nationality Law*. Jerusalem: Hebrew University Faculty of Law, 1970.

Harkavy, Robert. *Spectre of a Middle Eastern Holocaust: The Strategic and Diplomatic Implications of the Israeli Nuclear Weapons Program*. Denver, Co.: University of Denver Monograph Series, 1977.

Herzog, Chaim. *Who Stands Accused? Israel Answers Its Critics*. New York: Random House, 1978.

Howard, Esther. "Israel: The Sorcerer's Apprentice." *MERIP Reports* (February 1983).

Howe, Irving, and Carl Gershman. *Israel, the Arabs and the Middle East*. New York: Quadrangle Books, 1972.

International Organization for the Elimination of All Forms of Racism. *Zionism and Interstate Relations*. Tripoli, 1977.

Jabber, Fuad. *Israel and Nuclear Weapons: Present Options and Future Strategies*. London: Chatto & Windus for the International Institute for Strategic Studies, 1971.

Jiryis, Sabri. *The Arabs in Israel*. Beirut: Institute for Palestine Studies, 1969.

Kayyali, A. W., ed. *Zionism, Imperialism and Racism*. London: Croom Helm, 1979.

Khalidi, Walid. *From Haven to Conquest: Readings in Zionism and the Palestinian Problem Until 1948*. Beirut: The Institute for Palestine Studies, 1971.

Klieman, Aaron S. *Israel's Global Reach: Arms Sales as Diplomacy*. Washington: Pergamon-Brassey's, 1985.

Lumer, Hyman. *Zionism: Its Role in World Politics*. New York: International Publishers, 1973.

Lustick, Ian. *Arabs in the Jewish State: Israel's Control of a National Minority*. Austin: University of Texas Press, 1980.

Medzini, M., ed. *Israel's Foreign Relations*. Jerusalem: Israeli Foreign Ministry, 1979.

Meyer, Lawrence. *Israel Now: Portrait of a Troubled Land*. New York: Delacorte Press, 1982.

Peri, Yoram, and Amnon Neubach. *The Military-Industrial Complex in Israel: A Pilot Study*. Tel Aviv: International Center for Peace in the Middle East, 1985.

Perlmutter, Amos, et al. *Two Minutes Over Bagdad*. London: Vallentine, Mitchel & Co., 1982.

Perry, Victor. "Israel's Arm Exports." *Newsview* (Israel, November 7, 1984).

Pry, Peter. *Israel's Nuclear Arsenal*. Boulder, Co.: Westview Press, 1984.

Rodinson, Maxime. *Israel: A Colonial-Settler State?* New York: Monad Press, 1973.

Sacher, Howard. *A History of Israel*. New York: Alfred Knopf, 1981.

Safran, Nadav. *From War to War: The Arab-Israeli Confrontation 1948–1967*. Indianapolis, Ind.: The Bobbs-Merrill Co., 1969.

Said, Edward. *The Question of Palestine*. New York: Times Books, 1979.

Shahak, Israel. *The Non-Jew in the Jewish State: A Collection of Documents*. Edited and Published by Professor I. Shahak. Jerusalem, 1975.

———. *Israel's Global Role: Weapons for Repression*. Belmont, Mass.: Association of Arab-American University Graduates, 1981.

Shimoni, Yaakov. "Israel, the Arabs and Africa." *Africa Report* (July–August 1976).

Singh, Bhim. *An Examination of Documents on which the State of Israel is Based*. Beirut: PLO Research Center, 1970.

Smooha, Sammy, *Israel: Pluralism and Conflict*. Berkeley: University of California Press, 1978.

Smooha, Sammy and Don Peretz. "The Arabs in Israel," *The Journal of Conflict Resolution* (September 1982).

Weisbord, Robert G., and Richard Kazarian. *Israel in the Black American Perspective*. Westport, Conn.: Greenwood Press, 1985.

Weizmann, Chaim. *Trial and Error: The Autobiography of Chaim Weizmann*. New York: Random House, 1959.

Zureik, Elia T. *The Palestinians in Israel: A Study in Internal Colonialism*. London: Routledge & Paul 1979.

GENERAL WORKS

Betts, Richard K. "Paranoids, Pygmies, Pariahs, and Non-Proliferation." *Foreign Policy* (Spring 1977).

Cervenka, Zdenek. *The Organisation of African Unity and its Charter*. New York and Washington: Frederick A. Praeger, 1968.

Djanovich, Dusan J., ed. *United Nations Resolutions*. Dobbs Ferry, N.Y.: Oceana Publishers. Series I, vol. 8, 1960–1962.

Friedman, Julian. *Alliance in International Politics*. Boston: Allyn and Bacon, 1970.

Herz, John. *Political Realism and Political Idealism*. Chicago: University of Chicago Press, 1951.

International Monetary Fund. *Direction of Trade Statistics*. Washington, D.C., July 1982.

Jervis, Robert. *Perception and Misperception in International Politics*. Princeton, N.J.: Princeton University Press, 1976.

Liska, George. *Nations in Alliance: The Limits of Interdependence*. Baltimore: Johns Hopkins Press, 1962.

———. *Alliances and the Third World*. Baltimore: Johns Hopkins Press, 1968.

Marwah, Onkar, and Ann Schulz, eds. *Nuclear Proliferation and the Near Nuclear Countries*. Cambridge, Mass.: Ballinger Publishing Co., 1975.

Mazrui, Ali. "Black Africa and the Arab-Israeli Conflict." *Middle East International* (September 1978).

———. "Black Africa and the Arabs." *Foreign Affairs* (July 1975).

Morgenthau, Hans. *Politics Among Nations: The Struggle for Power and Peace*. New York: Knopf, 1960.

Pierre, Andrew. *The Global Politics of Arms Sales*. Princeton, N.J.: Princeton University Press, 1982.

Pretty, Ronald T. *Jane's Weapons Systems 1982–1983*. London: Jane's Publications, 1982.

Quester, George. *The Politics of Nuclear Proliferation*. Baltimore: Johns Hopkins Press, 1973.

————. *Nuclear Proliferation: Breaking the Chain*. Madison, Wis.: University of Wisconsin Press, 1981.

Richardson, Doug. *Naval Armaments*. London: Jane's Publications, 1981.

Schwab, George. *Ideology and Foreign Policy: A Global Perspective*. New York: Irvington, 1981.

Shaker, Mohamed I. *The Non-Proliferation Treaty*. Dobbs Ferry, N.Y.: Oceana Publishers, 1980.

Spector, Leonard. *Nuclear Proliferation Today*. Cambridge, Mass.: Ballinger, 1984.

————. "Proliferation: The Silent Spread." *Foreign Policy* no. 58 (Spring 1985).

Stockholm International Peace Research Institute. *World Armament and Disarmament. SIPRI Yearbook*. London: Taylor & Francis, Ltd., 1981.

Van den Berghe, Pierre. *Race and Racism: A Comparative Perspective*. New York: John Wiley and Sons, Inc., 1967.

Index

Abramowitz, Israel, 85-86
Adams, James, viii, ix, 4 n.1
Africa: apartheid, 2; decolonization of, 10; Israeli diplomacy and, 10-11, 18-19, 132; severing of diplomatic ties with Israel, 18-19; stance on Middle East conflict, 18; trade with South Africa, 32, 76-77; Vorster's visit to Israel, 28
African National Congress (ANC), 91, 125, 137
Afrikaner Resistance Movement, 82
Afrikaners: attitudes toward African majority, 120-21; and the Bible, 110-11; solidarity with Israel, 90-91; and World War II, 8, 9
Agmon, Tamir, 35
Agridev company, 37
Algeria, 18, 109
Aliens Act (South Africa), 8
Alon, Igal, 26
Amit, Gen. Meir, 44, 46
Anderson, Jack, 66, 67
Angola, 21, 47, 48, 56 n.41
Anti-Semitism, 105; South Africa, 8-10, 81-82
Apartheid, 1-2, 113; African con-

cern, 2; as anachronistic concept, 121-22; and the *Bible,* 110-11; early Israeli votes against, 11; Israeli boycott of UN votes on, 22, 145; Israeli declared opposition to, 10, 74, 98; Zionism, similarity to, 11-12, 90, 121-22
Apartheid legislation: Group Areas Act, 112; Immorality Act, 112; Liquor Act, 112; Pass Laws, 112; Population Registration Act, 112; Prohibition of Mixed Marriages Act, 112; Reservation of Separate Amenities Act, 112
Arecibo observatory, 65
Arens, Moshe, 134
Aridor, Yoram, 38, 95
Ariel, David, 99
Armaments Corporation of South Africa (ARMSCOR): "self suficiency" claims, 45-46, 49, 51, 78, 140
Arms transfers. *See* South Africa-Israel relations
Avineri, Shlomo, 93, 132

Balfour Declaration (1917), 7, 105
Bandung Conference (1955), 11

About the Author

BENJAMIN M. JOSEPH is currently Research Director at Claremont Research and Publications, a non-profit center for research on the Middle East, based in New York.